make it ™
yourself

Handcrafted
GIFTS

make it™
Yourself

Handcrafted
GIFTS

Make—and give—something beautiful and meaningful

weldon**owen**

Fabric & Sewing

001 adorn with ruffles
002 put a bow on it
003 contain essentials
004 nod to nautical style
005 create a galaxy
006 do a dip dye

4 Ways with Lace:

007 pretty up a pillow
008 judge a book by its cover
009 layer on a lace pocket
010 customize a table runner

011 create a notebook cover
012 wrap a journal
013 have a banner day
014 trim a tote bag
015 ruffle a twirly skirt
016 pretty up a pillow cover
017 spell it out

Felt

018 contain your jewels
019 give coasters the star treatment
020 pack up pencils
021 dress up a do
022 add fanciful flowers
023 upcycle a cozy bath mat

4 Ways to Gift a Pet:

024 wrap a package for rover
025 let doggie dine in style
026 play go fish with kitty
027 dress up your furry friend

028 add a touch of plush
029 connect the dots
030 create wall flowers

031 felt a table mat
032 put a ring on it
033 plant a no-water window box

Knit, Crochet & Knot

034 crochet a birdy basket
035 cozy up with a pint
036 fashion fingerless gloves
037 finger-knit a cowl
038 quick-crochet a button scarf

4 Ways to Gift a White Bowl:

039 wrap with rope
040 adorn with sequins
041 say it with clay
042 add a little gold leaf

043 join the band
044 string together flowers
045 make beautiful baskets
046 charm your friends
047 incite a chain reaction
048 go beyond bangles
049 bring your own bag
050 add flair with trims
051 tie up a trivet
052 polish a pillow
053 key in to creativity
054 twist a chew toy
055 knot a bracelet

Embroidery

056 stitch on scarves
057 string on sparkles
058 feather a nest
059 embroider fanciful florals
060 bring in the outdoors
061 give the key to your heart

Plants, Bouquets & Mini Gardens

Food Gifts

Crafting Basics & Patterns

NO GIFT YOU CAN BUY—no matter the price tag—has the unique sentiment of something you make with your own hands. Whether you enjoy crafting, are trying to be budget conscious, or simply want to create personalized presents for people you love, this book offers a variety of gift ideas for everyone in your life. From the simplest painted pot to more complex knitting projects or miniature gardens (and everything in between), the satisfaction you get from giving a gift that grew out of your time and creativity is unmatched—and you can be sure that whomever is lucky enough to receive your gift won't have anything else quite like it. When you make a gift, you make a memory.

the Editors

Fabric & Sewing

With a handful of basic supplies and simple sewing techniques, you can create handmade gifts for everyone on your list—whatever the occasion!

001
adorn with ruffles

Reimagine denim by turning it into a floral necklace highlighted with bits of bling. The flowers are made from layered denim circles accented with pearls in the centers. To make light and dark flowers, simply alternate which side of the denim is showing. Stitch the flowers to a ribbon, add necklace chain to the ends, and embellish with beads to finish.

YOU WILL NEED

8-inch square of denim: dark blue

Sewing thread: blue

Sewing needle

Assorted pearls

12-inch length of ½-inch-wide ribbon

15-inch-long necklace chains: two styles

Four jump rings

Jewelry pliers: round nose

Lobster clasp

Head pins

Assorted clear beads

1. Cut seven 1½-inch-diameter circles and five 2¼-inch-diameter circles from denim.

2. Fold a 2¼-diameter denim circle in half, then in half again to form a quarter circle. Using blue sewing thread, stitch through the folded pointed end of the circle with a few stitches to gather the center of the circle. Unfold the circle. Repeat with a 1½-inch-diameter circle.

3. Layer circles from Step 2 to make a flower. Stitch three pearls to the center, through all layers.

4. Repeat Steps 1–3 to make a total of five layered flowers. For a light blue flower, fold the circles with the dark side out. For a dark blue flower, fold the circles with the light side out.

Make three dark flowers and two light flowers.

5. Repeat Step 2 with two remaining 1½-inch-diameter denim circles to make two light blue single-layer flowers. Stitch one pearl to the center of each flower.

6. Lay ribbon on work surface. Pin denim flowers to the ribbon, alternating the light blue and dark blue flowers and slightly overlapping the flowers. Place a single-layer light blue flower on each end. Leave a 1-inch-long tail at each ribbon end. Stitch the flowers to the ribbon.

7. Thread a jump ring onto a ribbon end. Fold the ribbon back onto itself, and stitch to secure. Repeat on opposite ribbon end.

8. Cut each necklace chain into a 6-inch and a 9-inch length. Using jewelry pliers, open the jump ring from Step 7 and add both 6-inch chains to one jump ring and both 9-inch chains to the opposite jump ring. Close the jump rings.

9. Join the two chain ends on each side of the necklace with a jump ring. Add a lobster clasp to one ring.

10. Place a bead or pearl on a head pin. Using round-nose pliers, bend the wire on the head pin above the bead at a right angle. Cut wire to ⅜ inch long. Use pliers to bend the wire into a loop; insert wire through a necklace chain near the ribbon ends, then close the loop. Repeat with additional pearls and beads as desired.

002

put a bow on it

It's a wrap—a head wrap, that is! Sweet and sassy, this fabric headband with an elastic back makes a fun and feminine accessory.

YOU WILL NEED

3×16-inch rectangle of yellow-and-cream print (bow)

¼ yard of navy print (headband)

⅝-inch-wide elastic (3 inches for child, 5 inches for adult)

Chopstick or pencil

Large safety pin

Finished Headband:
  Adult: 1¾×21 inches
  Child: 1¾×17 inches

Yardages and cutting instructions are based on 42 inches of usable fabric width. Measurements include ¼-inch seam allowances. Sew with right sides together unless otherwise stated.

1. Cut pieces in the following order. Patterns are on the next page.

From the yellow-and-cream print, cut:
2 of Pattern A

From the navy print, cut:
1 of Pattern B (adult) or Pattern C (child)

2. Layer two yellow-and-cream Pattern A pieces with right sides together; pin. Sew together layered pieces along edges, starting at the middle and leaving a 1½-inch opening. At points, clip notches in seam allowance up to, but not through, stitching line (Diagram 1).

3. Turn right side out. Using a chopstick or eraser end of a pencil, gently push out ends. Press flat and slip-stitch opening closed to make a yellow-and-cream bow.

4. Layer two navy Pattern B or C pieces with right sides together. Using

½-inch seam allowance, sew together the top edges. Join the bottom edges (Diagram 2), leaving a 1½-inch opening, to make a tube.

5. Secure safety pin to one end of elastic and insert into a narrow end of tube. Work safety pin into tube until remaining elastic end aligns with tube opening. Sew across short end of tube to secure elastic (Diagram 3).

6. Pull safety pin through tube to opening at opposite end of tube. Remove safety pin and sew across end as before (Diagram 4).

7. Trim across corners at an angle close to the stitches. Turn tube right side out through opening on long edge, so that the elastic is on the outside of the headband. Press flat and slip-stitch opening closed to complete headband. Topstitch ⅛ inch from edge around entire tube.

8. Referring to photo, previous page, tie bow into knot around headband. Adjust as desired.

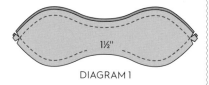

DIAGRAM 1

Make a matching set for a mom and daughter to wear as a pair.

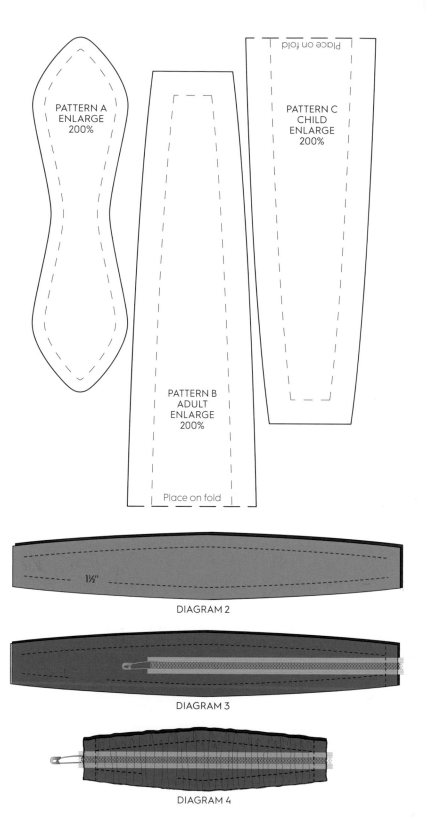

PATTERN A
ENLARGE
200%

PATTERN C
CHILD
ENLARGE
200%

Place on fold

PATTERN B
ADULT
ENLARGE
200%

Place on fold

1½"

DIAGRAM 2

DIAGRAM 3

DIAGRAM 4

003

contain essentials

Bring order to daily must-haves.

YOU WILL NEED

1 fat quarter (18×22½-inch) quilting weight cotton fabric

Medium weight fusible interfacing

Sewing thread

Sewing needle

Buttons

Pencil or air-soluble marking pen

Leather cording

1. Trace an 8½×11-inch sheet of paper onto a folded piece of fabric (the fold should be on one long edge of the rectangle), and cut out to create a piece that's 11×17 inches. Fold fabric in ¼ inch around all edges, wrong sides together, and press.

2. Cut one 8×10½-inch piece of fusible interfacing. Fold the fabric in half, right sides out, to create an 8¼×10½-inch rectangle, sandwiching the interfacing between the layers. Make sure the pressed edges are tucked under and align; press. Hand- or machine-stitch

along one short edge, knotting or backstitching the thread ends.

3. Fold up the stitched edge 4 inches to form the pocket of the fabric envelope, and press. Stitch around the sides and along the top edge. Fold top over, and press. Mark placement of two buttons about 1 inch apart with a pencil or air-soluble marking pen. Stitch on a 7-inch length of leather cording, then add one button to cover the stitch end of the cording. Add the second button and wrap the cording around to close.

004
nod to nautical style

Grommets and rope give these denim pillows a nautical vibe. Make each pillow by finishing the edges of two lightweight denim squares with an easy mitered double binding and 1-inch-diameter grommets. Sandwich a pillow form between the layers, and hold it together by tying short lengths of rope through the grommets.

YOU WILL NEED (for one pillow)

2¼ yards lightweight blue denim

Water-soluble marking pen

32—1-inch grommets

4½ yards sisal or rope

20-inch square pillow form

Yardages and cutting instructions are based on 42 inches of usable fabric width. Measurements include ½-inch seam allowances unless otherwise stated. Sew with right sides together unless otherwise stated.

Finished Pillow: 22×22 inches

CUT PIECES:

From lightweight blue denim, cut:
5—9×42-inch strips
2—19-inch squares

From sisal or rope, cut:
16—10-inch pieces

1. Using water-soluble marking pen, make a dot ½ inch from edges in all corners of both 19½-inch squares.

2. Join short ends of five 9×42-inch strips to make one long strip. Press seams open. Trim strip to 195 inches.

3. With the wrong side inside, fold under 1 inch at one end of a long strip (Diagram 1, next page). With wrong side inside, fold strip in half lengthwise to make a 4½×194-inch binding strip.

4. Beginning at a center raw edge of a marked square, align binding strip's raw edges with right side of marked square. Starting 2 inches from the folded end of strip, sew through all layers, ending stitching ½ inch (at dot) before reaching corner (Diagram 2, next page).

5. Fold binding strip up, making a diagonal fold; finger-press (Diagram 3, next page).

6. Hold Step 5 fold in place with your finger while bringing down binding strip in line with next pillow cover edge. (The horizontal fold aligns with the first raw edge of the large square.) Begin sewing again at the horizontal fold, stitching through all layers (Diagram 4, next page). ➲

HOW TO ADD A GROMMET

1. Mark location of grommet on the wrong side of fabric by placing grommet on the fabric and hitting it with a hammer. Using scissors, cut away the fabric within the circle. Slip the grommet through the right side of the fabric.

2. Place grommet on a hard surface. If you use a tabletop, protect the surface with a magazine. If you use concrete, the grommet may pick up texture. Place grommet top over grommet bottom with the fabric sandwiched between the pieces. Using a grommet-setting tool and a hammer, pound together the two pieces.

3. Check to make sure the pieces are tightly secured. Remove the grommet-setting tool.

7. Continue sewing binding around large square, turning corners in the same manner. When you return to starting point, trim end of binding strip as needed to tuck end inside folded end (Diagram 5). (Remaining binding is used for opposite side of pillow.)

8. Finish sewing to the starting point (Diagram 6).

9. Turn folded edge of binding to back of large square. Pin and press binding in place, making sure to cover the binding stitching line. Fold a miter in each corner as you reach it. **Note:** The binding will extend 2 inches beyond pillow center on all edges.

10. Topstitch the binding to the large square ⅛ inch from folded edge, making sure to cover the binding stitching line (Diagram 7). Topstitch again ¼ inch from first row of stitches. Repeat two rows of topstitching along outer edge of pillow cover.

11. Using water-soluble marking pen, center and mark a dot 4¼ inches from each corner on one edge of binding; make two additional dots, each 4½ inches from first dots. Repeat marking binding on each edge of pillow cover.

12. Referring to How to Add a Grommet, previous page, attach grommets centered on dots to complete one side of pillow cover (Diagram 8).

13. Repeat Steps 4–12 to make second side of pillow cover.

14. Sandwich pillow form between pillow covers. Thread sisal or rope through each set of corresponding grommets, and tie each with a square knot.

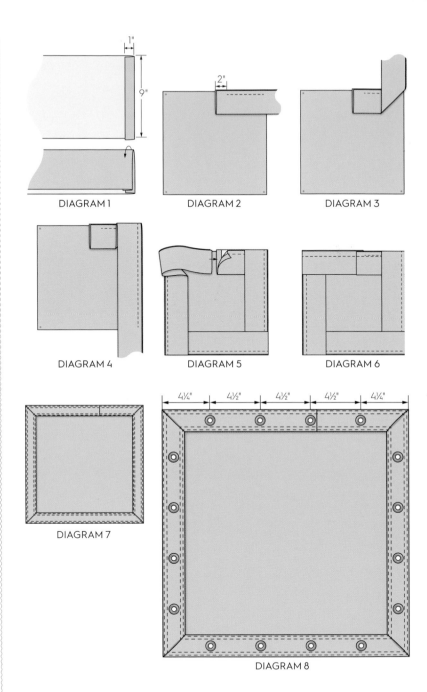

DIAGRAM 1

DIAGRAM 2

DIAGRAM 3

DIAGRAM 4

DIAGRAM 5

DIAGRAM 6

DIAGRAM 7

DIAGRAM 8

005
create a galaxy

Set a table with this interstellar needlework project.

YOU WILL NEED

Copyright-free galaxy illustration (vintage astronomy books are a good source at a high resolution)

8×10-inch printer paper

White cotton or linen fabric

Metallic embroidery floss

Embroidery needle

1. Scan the constellation illustration at a high resolution—at least 8×10 inches at 300 dpi.

2. Upload the image and have it printed on white cotton or linen fabric. (Our illustrations include solid-blue backgrounds and are printed on linen.)

3. Boost the runner's star power by highlighting with metallic embroidery floss. Silver and gold French knots add clusters of stars in the heavens. See #168 for details.

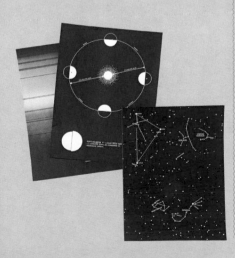

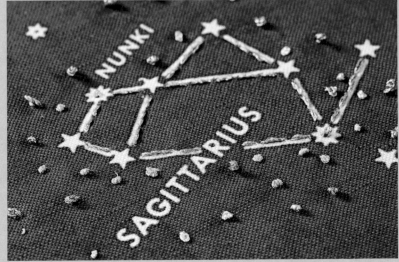

006
do a dip dye

A dyed throw and pillow wrap make a personalized gift with minimal effort. When working with large pieces of fabric, fold into a manageable size and use a clamp-style hanger to hold it while dipping the fabric into the dye. To make the pillow wrap, fray the edges of a fabric rectangle and accordion-fold the rectangle on a diagonal before putting it in the dye.

YOU WILL NEED
Indigo Tie Dye Kit
Bucket
Gloves
Plastic trash bag
Natural-fiber pillowcase or throw
Clamp-style pants hanger

1. Gather materials (A). Prepare indigo dye and let mixture set according to manufacturer's instructions. Spread plastic trash bag on surface where the wet fabric will hang to drip.

2. Soak fabric in water, squeeze to remove excess, and fold fabric to fit in hanger (B). Dip a portion of the fabric into dye (C). Lift and lower the fabric in the dye until satisfied with dyed edge and intensity of color (D).

3. Rinse fabric, unfold, and hang. Let dye drip onto trash bag. Heat-set in a dryer.

4 Ways with Lace

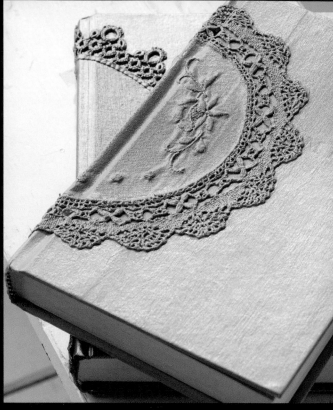

007
pretty up a pillow

Breathe life into a ho-hum linen pillow with scraps of trim. Fabric stores often have grab bags of bits and pieces, and etsy.com is a treasure trove of gorgeous remnants. For this look, mix lace trims cut to fit the width of the pillow. Use a hot-glue gun to adhere the remnants, then let cool. For an eclectic and elegant look, dress up pillows in varying sizes with trim scraps in the same color family, then toss three or four onto a sofa or bed.

008
judge a book by its cover

Cover old books with a monochrome doily design. To start, dip a doily into a 3-to-1 mixture of decoupage medium to water, then lay across the spine of the book and smooth outward. Using a foam brush, soak up drips and let dry on waxed paper. Next, apply a couple coats of acrylic paint. Let dry.

009
layer on a lace pocket

Freshen up a tote with a lace embellishment that doubles as a pocket. To begin, cut a piece of wide lace, leaving an inch or so extra on three sides to finish the edges. Using a stencil brush, cover more than half of the lace with a punchy acrylic paint (we opted for a pretty pink hue), then finish the rest with a metallic gold paint. (Bonus: Score two DIY projects in one! Slip a piece of cream paper behind the lace as you paint—the lace will act as a stencil and leave you with a beautifully printed paper ideal for wrapping gifts or making cards.) Once dry, place the painted lace on the tote bag, folding under the side and bottom edges and securing with hot glue or stitching.

010
customize a table runner

This eyelet-inspired runner brings a bit of boho flare to the table. Cut an 18-inch width of light gray felt to fit your dining room table. Using a fabric marking pen, trace a leaf pattern in an eyelet design on half the runner. Cut out the shapes, then fold the runner in half and mark the pattern on the other side to ensure the design is symmetrical. Cut out. Hot-glue a same-size sheet of lace to the underside, then finish the short edges by hot-gluing on a fun fabric trim or coordinating piece of fabric.

011
create a notebook cover

Embellish a standard composition notebook with fabric squares and contrasting stitches.

YOU WILL NEED

7½×9¾-inch composition book
⅜ yard of solid cream fabric
Fabric scraps: blue and taupe
Fusible web
Water-soluble marking pen
Acrylic ruler
Embroidery floss: blue and taupe
16×10½-inch piece of fusible interfacing

Measurements include ¼-inch seam allowances unless otherwise stated. Sew with right sides together unless otherwise stated.

CUT PIECES

From solid cream fabric, cut:
1—10½×16-inch rectangle (body)
2—6½×10½-inch rectangles (pockets)
1—10½×6-inch rectangle (lining)

From fusible interfacing, cut:
10½×16-inch rectangle (body lining)
2—6×10-inch rectangles (pocket linings)

1. Trace the square pattern, right, onto white paper. Trace pattern five times onto paper side of fusible web, leaving 1 inch between squares. Cut out around squares.

2. With the fusible side down, press three fusible-web shapes onto back side of blue fabric scrap and two fusible-web shapes onto back side of taupe fabric scrap. Cut out squares on the lines.

3. Fold the 16×10½-inch solid cream in half crosswise to measure 8×10½ inches. Using a water-soluble marking pen and an acrylic ruler, draw a line 2 inches from the folded edge (Diagram 1).

4. Remove paper from fusible-web squares and center squares along drawn line so points touch end to end, alternating blue and taupe squares (Diagram 2). Press shapes.

5. Using two strands of taupe embroidery floss, blanket-stitch around edges of each square. See #168 for stitch instructions.

6. Using three strands of blue embroidery floss, stitch running stitches through centers of squares in a straight line from top to bottom edges of fabric. Stitch an outline of running stitches approximately ¼ inch outside left and right sides of squares. Stitch a second outline on right side of squares that is ¼ inch outside the first outline stitches.

7. Turn one long edge under of a 6½×10½-inch solid cream pocket piece by ¼ inch, then turn under by another ¼-inch (Diagram 3).

8. Using an iron, fuse the 16×10½-inch pocket lining to wrong side of embroidered 16×10½-inch body piece. Fuse a 6×10½-inch pocket lining to wrong side of each pocket piece.

9. With wrong sides together, place pocket units on embroidered body piece, aligning outside raw edges. Place lining on center top, aligning the top and bottom raw edges (Diagram 4). Sew pieces together around outside edges. Clip corners and turn right side out.

10. Insert journal cover into pockets. **Note:** If necessary, cover original journal cover with white paper to prevent show-through.

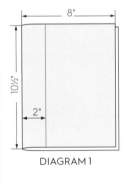

DIAGRAM 1

DIAGRAM 2

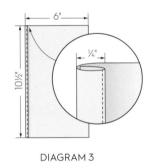

DIAGRAM 3

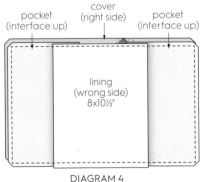

pocket (interface up)   cover (right side)   pocket (interface up)

lining (wrong side) 8x10½"

DIAGRAM 4

SQUARE PATTERN

012

wrap a journal

Use colorful strips of jersey to transform a plain notebook into a pretty present.

YOU WILL NEED

Strips of jersey cotton (or T-shirts)

Sewing thread

Hand-sewing needle or sewing machine

Scissors

Kraft paper notebook

Hot-glue gun and glue sticks

Tie a series of knots in a strip of jersey and wrap it around the notebook. Or stitch a length of fabric and pull ends of thread to gather as desired. Glue in place to finish.

013
have a banner day

Whether for a birthday or any day, swag this happy-go-lucky scallop banner to get the party started.

Finished Banner: Approximately 8½ feet long with nine scallops.

Fabrics are 44 to 45 inches wide. Sew with ¼-inch seam allowances and right sides together.

YOU WILL NEED

9—8×16-inch pieces of assorted coordinating fabrics
Rotary cutter
Acrylic ruler
Straight pins
3 yards double-fold seam binding
Matching sewing thread

1. Cut a 7-inch diameter circle from a sheet of white paper. Cut one 8×16-inch fabric piece in half to make two 8-inch squares. Lay circle template on wrong side of one 8-inch fabric square. Trace around template with a pencil. Pin squares with right sides together and traced circle on top.

2. Join pieces by machine-stitching on drawn line, overlapping beginning and ending stitches to complete circle. Sew slowly to ensure circle has no bumps or points. Trim fabric ⅛ inch outside stitched line.

3. Fold circle in half; crease. Cut along crease with rotary cutter and acrylic ruler to create two half-circles or scallops. Turn scallops right side out, using your finger to poke out

curve. Press edge with iron to get a perfect curved edge.

4. Repeat Steps 1 through 3 with remaining 8×16-inch fabric pieces to make a total of nine scallops.

5. Open double-fold seam binding on work surface. Place first scallop 14 inches from one end, positioning scallop so top edge meets inner fold of seam binding; pin. Continue pinning

scallops to tape, spacing each one 1½ inches apart.

6. Using matching sewing thread and beginning 1 inch from end of binding, stitch a ⅛-inch seam along open edge, securing each scallop as you sew length of binding. Sew 14 inches past last scallop, and backstitch at end before trimming thread. Trim binding ends at an angle.

014
trim a tote bag

Turn a blank ready-made tote bag into a canvas for colorful fabric scallops and embroidered details.

YOU WILL NEED

13×13½-inch white canvas tote bag

Water-soluble marking pen

Acrylic ruler

Assorted fabric scraps: light blue, taupe, orange

Lightweight fusible web

Embroidery floss: taupe, orange, light blue

Embroidery needle

5 or 6—¾-inch-diameter buttons to coordinate with fabrics

Sewing thread: white

Spray bottle filled with water

1. Lay tote bag on work surface with bottom edge folded flat. Using water-soluble marking pen and an acrylic ruler, mark a straight line 3¾ inches above bottom folded edge across front of bag. Mark a second straight line ¼ inch below first marked line and a third straight line ⅝ inch below first marked line (Diagram 1).

2. Using a pencil, trace the half-moon pattern, right, onto white paper and cut out. Trace pattern six times onto paper side of fusible web, leaving 1-inch space between shapes. Leaving about ¼ inch outside the lines, cut around fusible-web shapes.

3. Using an iron and following fusible web manufacturer's instructions, press two fusible-web pieces onto back of each fabric scrap. Cut out each shape on the lines for a total of six half-moons.

4. Remove paper backing from each half-moon shape. Place shapes along top marked line on bag with straight edges of each shape on the line and the curved side extending above line. Press shapes with an iron (Diagram 2).

5. Using two strands of taupe embroidery floss, blanket-stitch around edges of each half-moon shape. See #168 for embroidery diagrams and instructions.

6. Using the water-soluble marking pen and the ruler, mark a scallop line ¼-inch around the curved portions of each half-moon shape on bag front.

7. Use six strands of embroidery floss and a running stitch for all embroidery. Stitch scallop line above half-moon

shapes with orange embroidery floss. Stitch first line below half-moon shapes with light blue embroidery floss. Stitch second straight line with taupe embroidery floss.

8. Using a water-soluble marking pen and the ruler, center and mark two parallel lines on each strap, spacing them ½ inch apart. Stitch lines with light blue floss.

9. Using white sewing thread, stitch a button to center of each half-moon shape. If you like, leave a button off a shape to allow fabric print to show.

10. Lightly mist fabric with water to remove visible water-soluble marking pen lines. Let fabric dry. Press dry fabric with an iron set to a no-steam setting.

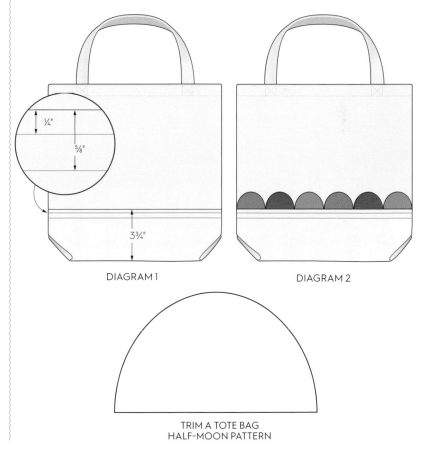

DIAGRAM 1

DIAGRAM 2

TRIM A TOTE BAG
HALF-MOON PATTERN

015

ruffle a twirly skirt

Dress up your favorite girlie girl in a bouncy multilayered skirt.

YOU WILL NEED

¾-inch-wide elastic (for all sizes)

For girls' sizes 3/4, 5/6, 7/8:
½ yard floral
½ yard polka dot

For girls' size 9/10:
¾ yard floral
¾ yard polka dot

Finished Skirts:

Size 3/4: 10⅛ inches long
Size 5/6: 13⅛ inches long
Size 7/8: 16⅛ inches long
Size 9/10: 19⅛ inches long

Yardages and cutting instructions are based on 42 inches of usable fabric width. Measurements include ¼-inch seam allowances. Sew with right sides together unless otherwise stated.

CUT PIECES:

SIZE 3/4

From floral, cut:
2—6¼×24½-inch rectangles for upper ruffle
2—5×13-inch rectangles for upper band

From polka dot, cut:
2—4¾×24½-inch rectangles for lower ruffle
2—3¼×13-inch rectangles for lower band

SIZE 5/6

From floral, cut:
2—7¼×25-inch rectangles for upper ruffle
2—6×13½-inch rectangles for upper band

From polka dot, cut:
2—5¾×25-inch rectangles for lower ruffle
2—4¼×13½-inch rectangles for lower band

SIZE 7/8

From floral, cut:
2—8¼×25½-inch rectangles for upper ruffle
2—7×14-inch rectangles for upper band

From polka dot, cut:
2—6¾×25½-inch rectangles for lower ruffle
2—5¼×14-inch rectangles for lower band

SIZE 9/10

From floral, cut:
2—9¼×26-inch rectangles for upper ruffle
2—8×14½-inch rectangles for upper band

From polka dot, cut:
2—7¾×26-inch rectangles for lower ruffle
2—6¼×14½-inch rectangles for lower band

1. Sew together upper band floral rectangles along narrow edges to make a tube (Diagram 1). Press seams open.

2. Join upper ruffle floral rectangles along short edges to make a ruffle tube. Press seams open. Turn under ¼ inch on one long edge of ruffle tube; press. Turn under a second time ¼ inch; press. To hem, sew through all layers close to first folded edge.

3. With a long machine-basting stitch, sew ¼ inch from long raw edge of ruffle tube. Pull threads to gather edge.

4. With right sides together, align bottom edge of upper band and gathered edge of ruffle tube (Diagram 2); match seams and adjust ruffle to fit band. Pin and stitch to make upper skirt unit. Press seam toward upper band.

5. Repeat Steps 1–4 using lower band polka dot rectangles and lower ruffle polka dot rectangles to make lower skirt unit.

6. With raw edges aligned, match seams of right side of lower band with wrong side of upper ruffle where upper band and upper ruffle are joined; sew through all layers (Diagram 3); press.

7. Turn under raw edge of upper band ½ inch; press. Turn under a second time 1⅛ inch; press.

8. Sew through all layers close to the first folded edge, leaving a 2-inch opening for inserting elastic (Diagram 4).

9. Insert elastic and adjust to fit. Sew ends of elastic together. Sew opening closed. Turn right side out to complete skirt.

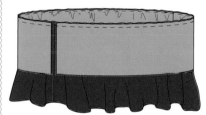

DIAGRAM 1

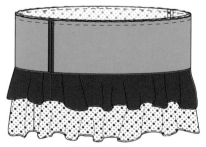

DIAGRAM 2

DIAGRAM 3

DIAGRAM 4

016
pretty up a pillow cover

Design a prismatic pillow cover to dress up even the most basic furniture. Customize colors for a specific palette or color preference.

YOU WILL NEED

Cardstock

Ruler

Pencil

Scissors

Felt, in assorted colors

White pillow cover

Throw pillow insert

Fabric glue or iron-on adhesive

Embroidery floss in coordinating colors

Embroidery needle

1. Make a triangle template with the cardstock. Trace and cut out triangles from felt. Attach them to the pillow cover with fabric glue or iron-on adhesive. Let dry or set completely.

2. Highlight the shapes with long stitches in coordinating embroidery floss. See #168.

Crafty Headboard: Craft a driftwood-look headboard by staining pine boards in three diluted shades of black glaze. (We used Wood Icing Furniture Glazing Color in Licorice.) Once dry, arrange the boards in a basket-weave pattern on the floor, then attach them to the wall with pin nails. Paint edges gold.

017

spell it out

Turn simple cut-out letters into custom pillows fit for friends, family, or your own home.

YOU WILL NEED

Store-bought pillowcase

Quilting weight cotton fabric

Scissors

Fusible interfacing

Cut out letters as desired. Arrange onto pillowcase and secure with fusible webbing, according to manufacturer's directions.

Felt

Soft and naturally cozy, felt is as versatile as it is easy to work with.
Try your hand at making a range of projects, then spread your
creativity around by gifting to friends.

018
contain your jewels

Thick felt is a little more difficult to cut but is generally sturdier and smoother than thin felt—and it's perfect for this stylish catchall.

YOU WILL NEED
3-millimeter-thick felt sheet
Scissors
Packing tape
Sewing needle
Hand sewing thread

1. Fold a piece of paper in half and cut using the pattern on Pattern Page A. Use packing tape on the underside to attach the pattern to the felt sheet (A).

2. Cut out the felt shape using sharp scissors; notch each corner, stopping at the marked point on the pattern.

3. Pinch the cut corners and sew using a straight stitch and matching thread (B).

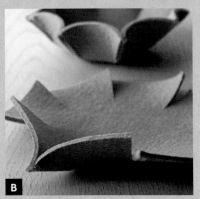

019

give coasters the star treatment

Dense wool felt—usually found on a bolt and purchased by the yard—is ideal for heavy-use items such as these sophisticated coasters.

YOU WILL NEED

Felt in assorted colors

Paper-backed fusible web (such as Wonder-Under)

Packing tape

1. Trace the patterns from Pattern Page A. Trace and cut out from neutral-color felt and paper-backed fusible web. Apply the fusible web to the corresponding felt shapes.

2. Cut diamonds from a variety of felt colors, using packing tape to hold the patterns in place (A). Remove the paper backing from the fusible web of the star shape to expose the adhesive, and then fuse the diamonds in place on the star (B). Fuse the circle to the back of each coaster for added padding (C).

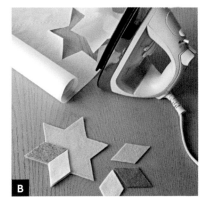

020

pack up pencils

Practical for kids, pretty enough for adults, this felt pencil roll is easily customized. This one holds 20 pencils.

YOU WILL NEED
14×13½-inch piece of felt
Sewing machine
Coordinating thread
Disappearing ink pen

1. Fold over the bottom edge of the felt ½ inch and stitch. Fold the bottom with the hem to the inside to form a 14×8½-inch roll; sew the sides using ½-inch seam allowances.

2. Mark small equal-size pockets for each pencil (A). Sew along each line, backstitching at the beginning and end of each row for durability.

3. To make a tie, sew a 9×1½-inch felt strip to the pencil roll edge (B).

021
dress up a do

These bow barrettes are so easy to make, you can craft a set in minutes.

YOU WILL NEED

12×18-inch sheet of wool felt

7-inch length of ¾-inch-wide glitter ribbon (optional)

Hot-glue gun and glue sticks

Metal alligator hair clip

From wool felt, cut:

1—1⅜×7½-inch strip
1—1⅜×4-inch strip
1—1⅝×2½-inch rectangle

1. Hot-glue the short ends of the 1⅜×7½-inch wool felt strip together to make a loop. **Note:** If you would like a glitter-ribbon layer on your bow, hot-glue glitter ribbon to the wool felt strip before gluing the strip into a loop.

2. Pinch loop in center, centering glued seam at back; hot-glue front and back together to make loops.

3. Cut a V-shape notch on each end of the 1⅜×4-inch wool felt strip using scissors. Hot-glue pinched portion of bow loops to center top of notched wool felt strip.

4. Wrap the 1⅝×2½-inch wool felt piece around center of bow and hot-glue on back.

5. Hot-glue a metal alligator hair clip to the back of the bow.

022
add fanciful flowers

Top off your look with a ribbon belt trimmed with a trio of felt flowers. Each flower is made from a fringed felt strip that's been rolled and glued to a length of grosgrain ribbon.

YOU WILL NEED

⅛ yard each of 36-inch-wide felt: gold, dark red, cream, forest green

1½-inch-wide grosgrain ribbon (enough to fit around waist with ribbon ends tied in a bow): brown

Hot-glue gun and glue sticks

1. Cut a 3½×5-inch rectangle from forest green felt. Find center of ribbon length, and hot-glue center of ribbon to center of felt rectangle. Fold felt rectangle around ribbon, sandwiching the ribbon between the felt layers. Hot-glue in place.

2. Cut a 1×36-inch strip from red, gold, or cream felt. Cut ¾-inch-deep slits along length of strip, spacing slits approximately ¼ inch apart. Roll strip tightly, placing a dab of hot glue every 6 inches along uncut edge to hold roll together. Use fingertips to spread out cut strips and fluff flower.

3. Repeat Step 2 with each felt color to make a total of three flowers.

4. Trace leaf pattern, left, onto white paper; cut out. Cut four leaves from forest green felt. Referring to pattern, cut slit at end of each leaf. To add dimension, overlap slit edges and hot-glue the pieces together.

5. Hot-glue leaves and flowers to belt, tucking petals underneath flowers with the overlapped leaf edges positioned under flowers.

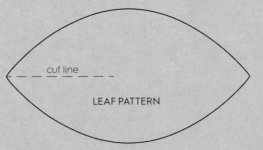

cut line

LEAF PATTERN

023

upcycle a cozy bath mat

Super soft and super pretty, this 21×31-inch bath mat recycles discarded cable-knit sweaters into a cozy floor cover.

YOU WILL NEED

Wool sweaters: blue, cream, blue plaid

Felting needle punch tool and brush mat

Five 18-inch strands of three-ply pink wool yarn

1. Felt the sweaters (see #170). Cut 6-inch-diameter circles, 12 blue and 12 cream.

2. Lay out a row of six circles, alternating the colors; overlap the circles 1 inch, keeping the blue circles on top of the cream circles. Lay out the second, third, and fourth rows of circles in the same way, alternating colors in the row and between the rows, creating a checkerboard effect. The rows should overlap each other 1 inch, and the blue circles should always be on top. **Note:** There should be openings between the circles. Use the needle-punch felting tool to join the circles.

3. Trace the star pattern, right, and cut 15 stars from the plaid wool. Position the stars over the openings between the circles. Use the needle-punch felting tool to attach the stars to the circles.

4. Separate the three-ply wool yarn. Wind one ply of yarn in a solid circle in the center of each star; attach the yarn to the stars using the needle-punch felting tool.

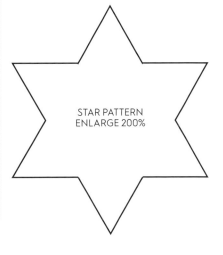

STAR PATTERN
ENLARGE 200%

4 Ways to Gift a Pet

024
wrap a package for rover

Cut out desired image from photo. Use a photocopier to print and cut out multiple copies of the same image. Glue the images to a sheet of paper and photocopy this template to create wrapping paper. Using a crafts knife, cut a square in a piece of folded corrugated paper or cardstock to form a frame on the gift card. Tape an image from the printed wrap to the inside of the card opening. Hot-glue two bone-shape treats or toys to the tag, aligning one above the other. Cut slits the same width as the ribbon above and below the top bone and below the bottom bone. Working from front to back, slide a ribbon end through each slit near the top bone. Slide both ends of the ribbon from back to front through the slit near the bottom bone. Glue the ribbon in place; trim the ends. Write the pet's name on the bottom bone. The bones are not meant to be eaten.

025
let doggie dine in style

This simple disguise refashions pet dishes in a beautiful decor piece. Place two metal dog food bowls right side up on a lidded rectangular basket and trace around the bottoms. To cut out the circles, drill a hole inside each circle and insert a jigsaw. Cut around the inside edge of the marked circles. Drop the bowl into the hole. The edge of the opening should catch the lip of the bowl. If a hole is too small, shave off the edge in small increments using the jigsaw.

026
play go fish with kitty
Trace patterns on Pattern Page B onto felt; cut out. Embroider details as desired. Using manufacturer's directions, add fusible web to the wrong sides of the

027
dress up your furry friend
Dress up your favorite animal friend with a festive bandanna. Cut jersey knit cotton into a triangle (ours is 21×21×33 inches) to fit your furry buddy, and use a pencil

028
add a touch of plush

Each petal is cut from a solid-color sweater or sweatshirt and then arranged and stitched to a neutral sweater background.

YOU WILL NEED

3 sweaters (1 neutral and 2 contrasting colors)

Lightweight iron-on fusible stabilizer or interfacing

Crafts glue (optional)

16-inch-square pillow form or polyester fiberfill

CUT THE PIECES

From neutral sweater, cut:
2—17-inch squares

From each contrasting color sweater, cut:
8 of Petal Pattern (right)

From stabilizer or interfacing, cut:
1—16½-inch square

1. Following manufacturer's instructions, iron the fusible stabilizer 16½-inch square to wrong side of one neutral sweater 17-inch square.

2. Referring to Diagram 1, arrange eight matching petals on right side of interfaced 17-inch square; place centers of petals about 2 inches apart. Pin petals in place, then sew about ¼ inch from edges of each petal with thread to match petals. Repeat to arrange and sew remaining eight matching petals in place; these petals should each overlap each other (Diagram 2).

3. With right sides together, layer pillow top and remaining neutral sweater 17-inch square. Leaving an opening in the center of one edge, sew together using a ½-inch seam. Sew over all edges with a machine zigzag stitch for stability. Trim across corners in order to turn corners out completely. Turn right side out.

4. To create the middle of the flower, make a sweater pom-pom or choose a very large button. Sew or glue on flower pom-pom or button. Stuff with pillow form or fiberfill. Sew opening closed to complete pillow.

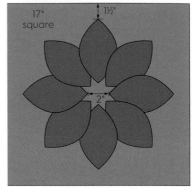

DIAGRAM 1

DIAGRAM 2

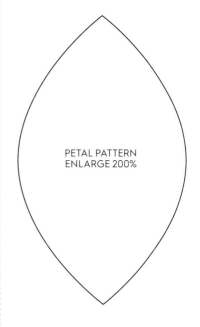

PETAL PATTERN
ENLARGE 200%

HOW TO MAKE A SWEATER POM-POM

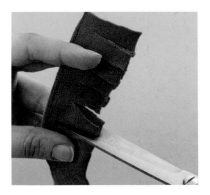

1. Fold a 3×16-inch sweater strip in half lengthwise. Sew about ⅛ inch from fold. Make 1-inch-deep cuts every ¼–½ inch along the length of the strip.

2. Roll strip tightly in a spiral while holding it tightly along the sewn edge. Fan out the cut edge. Secure rolled back side with a pin and glue.

029
connect the dots

Made of felt and baker's twine, this simple garland easily gets little family members in on the crafting fun.

YOU WILL NEED
Lightweight cardboard
Freezer paper
Wool felt: red, light blue, and light green
Baker's twine
Fabric glue

1. Trace pattern below onto tracing paper; cut out. Trace patterns onto lightweight cardboard; cut out.

2. Using an iron on medium heat, press freezer paper, shiny side down, onto felt. Trace patterns on the freezer paper. Cut out circles and peel off freezer paper. **Note:** To save time, cut circles from two sheets of felt layered together, one without freezer paper.

3. Cut baker's twine to desired length of the garland. Sandwich together two matching-color circles with the baker's twine in-between. Glue together the circles using fabric glue. Continue adding circles to the twine, alternating colors and spacing circles about ¾ inch apart, until garland is filled with felt circles.

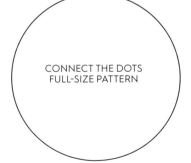

CONNECT THE DOTS
FULL-SIZE PATTERN

030
create wall flowers

Give someone a seasonal wall corsage—green thumb not required! Let extras bloom on pillows, a wreath, and holiday packages.

YOU WILL NEED

Lightweight cardboard

Freezer paper

Wool felt: white, dark red, and red

Fabric glue

Clip clothespins

Hole punch

Removable double-sided tape

1. Trace patterns on Pattern Page A onto tracing paper; cut out. Trace patterns onto lightweight cardboard; cut out.

2. Using an iron on medium heat, press freezer paper, shiny side down, onto felt. Tracing patterns on the freezer paper, trace Large Poinsettia and Large Leaf onto white felt, Small Poinsettia onto dark red felt, and Small Leaf onto red felt the number of times indicated on patterns. Cut out shapes and peel off freezer paper.

3. Dab fabric glue on right side of one corner of leaf; pinch together, holding in place with a clothespin. Repeat for each leaf. Let glue dry; remove clothespins. Apply fabric glue to back of leaf; glue to poinsettia between petals. Repeat with other leaves. Use a hole punch to punch five dots from white felt for red flower and five dots from red felt for white flower. Glue a dot over glued seam of each folded petal. Adhere flowers to wall with removable double-sided tape.

031
felt a table mat

Would you believe that this lacy table mat is completely no-sew? White felt shapes are joined together with repeated pokes from a needle-felting tool and then accented with needle-felted dots of colored wool roving.

YOU WILL NEED

½ yard of 72-inch-wide ivory felt

Water-soluble marking pen

Needle-felting mat

Needle-felting tool

Wool roving: mint green and red

Finished Mat: Approximately 21 inches square.

1. Trace the patterns onto white paper; cut out. From ivory felt, cut 40 large petals and 36 small petals.

2. Place four large petals on the needle-felting mat so one end of each petal overlaps in the center to make a plus shape. Using the needle-felting tool, poke the intersection repeatedly to meld the fibers, joining the pieces (B). Felt three more petals to one of the petals from the first plus shape to make a second adjoining plus shape. Referring to the photo, opposite, continue adding petals to make a four-by-four grid of large petal shapes.

3. Repeat Step 2 with four small petals. Make nine small x shapes with four small petals each. Referring to the photograph, opposite, position a small x shape into each of the square openings in the four-by-four grid of large petal shapes. Use the needle-felting tool to felt the tips of each small x shape to the large petal plus shapes.

4. Pull off a small tuft of red wool roving and place it in the center of one of the large plus shapes. Use the needle-felting tool to poke the roving into a ½-inch-wide circle. Repeat at each large plus intersection.

5. Repeat Step 4 using a small tuft of mint green wool roving in the center of each of the small x shapes (C). Felt the roving into a circle slightly smaller than the red felted circles.

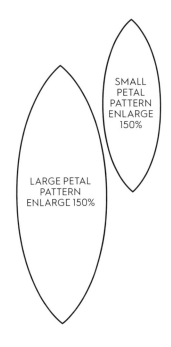

SMALL PETAL PATTERN ENLARGE 150%

LARGE PETAL PATTERN ENLARGE 150%

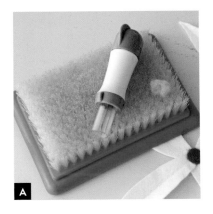

A

B

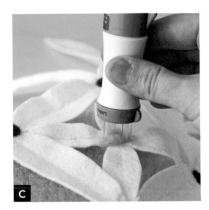

C

032

put a ring on it

Complete the gift with napkin rings that coordinate with the table mat, left. Fold and pinch felt petal shapes, and glue them together at the center to form each flower. Top each with a small needle-felted ball.

YOU WILL NEED

8×11-inch pieces of felt: white, ivory, mint green

Hot-glue gun and glue sticks

Wool roving: sea foam green and red

Needle-felting mat

1. Trace the small petal pattern, opposite page, onto white paper; cut out. Cut eight petals from white or ivory felt.

2. Fold each petal in half lengthwise; press the fold. Pinch the petal in the center and hot-glue the petal edges together at the center to keep the pinched shape. Repeat with seven more petals. Hot-glue petals together at the centers to form a flower.

3. Cut a 2×8-inch strip from mint green or ivory felt. Hot-glue ends together to form a ring. **Note:** Dry-fit the ring around the napkin and adjust the size as necessary before gluing the ends together. Hot-glue flower to center front of napkin ring.

4. Using red or sea foam wool roving, follow the instructions, opposite, to make a dense ⅜-inch-diameter felted ball. Hot-glue the ball to the center of each flower.

033
plant a no-water window box

Wool felt makes this grouping of desert succulents strikingly lifelike. Whip up as many of the six succulents as necessary to fit inside your container, and have fun changing the colors for a custom arrangement. Follow the instructions for each individual succulent, then arrange according to the instructions in Steps 1 through 3.

YOU WILL NEED
Tracing paper
Wool-blend felt: heather purple, seafoam green, olive green, sage green, heather gray, aqua
Hot-glue gun and glue sticks
4½×12-inch wood box

Floral foam block (such as FloraCraft)
Foam cutter (such as FloraCraft)
Artificial moss
18-gauge florists wire

1. Use the foam cutter to cut a piece of floral foam to fit the inside of the box. Glue foam into box.

2. Cover the top of the foam block with artificial moss. Cut 15 to 20 5-inch lengths from florists wire. Bend each wire into a U-shape, then insert the pins through the moss and into the foam block to secure the moss.

3. Determine arrangement of the succulents. Secure each succulent in the box by sliding a U-pin around a leaf or wrapping it around the stem.

Succulent 1: Trace patterns on Pattern Page D onto tracing paper; cut out. Place a dab of hot glue at the point of each leaf; pinch leaf ends. Glue leaves together along the pinched ends.

Succulent 2: Trace patterns on Pattern Page D onto tracing paper; cut out. Place a dab of hot glue in the center of each leaf cluster; pinch the centers to gather. Stack leaves from largest to smallest, gluing the layers together at the center. Stack the clusters and rotate the layers so they're offset. Glue the layers together at the center.

Succulent 3: Trace patterns on Pattern Page D onto tracing paper; cut out. Run a line of hot glue along one long edge of the stem piece. Roll the piece into a long tube for the stem; let dry. Glue two large leaves opposite each other near the base of the stem. Working up the stem, add two more pairs of large leaves, spacing them ¾ inch apart. Glue two medium leaves ¼ inch from the top end of the stem, then add smallest leaves to the top.

Succulent 4: Trace patterns on Pattern Page D onto tracing paper; cut out. Place a dab of hot glue at the bottom of a leaf; pinch the leaf to gather the end. Repeat with each leaf. Glue the gathered ends of each leaf together.

Succulent 5: Trace patterns on Pattern Page D onto tracing paper; cut out. Overlap the slit ends of a cut leaf, and hot-glue them together to create a gathered end. Repeat for all leaves with slits. Glue leaves of each size together to form clusters. Working from largest to smallest, stack the clusters and rotate to offset layers. Glue the layers together at the center.

Succulent 6: Trace patterns on Pattern Page D onto tracing paper; cut out. Run a line of hot glue along one long edge of the stem; fold stem in half. Beginning at the top, hot-glue smallest leaves around stem. Continue hot-gluing leaves down the stem, overlapping larger leaves and as you work your way down the stem. Leave ½ inch uncovered at the bottom of the stem.

Knit, Crochet & Knot

Make personal accessories, home decorations, and more for giving with the pretty texture of knitting, crochet stitches, and knotting. Try a new skill or expand your current repertoire.

034
crochet a birdy basket

Work up this owl basket in rounds of half double crochet, then crochet each eye piece, and sew the pieces to the body. Embroider the beak between the eyes using yarn and a tapestry needle.

YOU WILL NEED

2—5-ounce skeins worsted weight yarn: gray (such as Red Heart Super Saver in Grey Heather)

Size J crochet hook

Blunt-end yarn needle

Gauge: 6 rows and 8 hdc = 3 inches

Note: See #169.

Finished Basket: 8 inches tall

ABBREVIATIONS

hdc-inc, dc-inc, sc-inc = work two of the designated st in one stitch.

hdc-dec = (Yo, insert hook in next st, yo and draw up a lp) twice, yo and draw through all 5 lps on hook.

picot = ch 5, sl st in top of first st.

CROCHET THE BASKET

Note: The basket is worked in a spiral, so joining rounds is not necessary. Mark beginning of each round. See #169.

Rnd 1: With 2 strands of yarn held together, ch 3 (2 chs counts as hdc), hdc 7 times in beg ch (8 hdc).

Rnd 2: Hdc-inc in each st (16 hdc).

Rnd 3: *Hdc-inc, hdc in next st; rep from * 7 more times (24 hdc).

Rnd 4: *Hdc-inc, hdc in next 2 sts; rep from * 7 more times (32 hdc).

Rnd 5: *Hdc-inc, hdc in next 3 sts; rep from * 7 more times (40 hdc).

Rnd 6: *Hdc-inc, hdc in next 4 sts; rep from * 7 more times (48 hdc).

Rnd 7: * Hdc-inc, hdc in next 5 sts; rep from * 7 more times (56 hdc).

Rnd 8: * Hdc-inc, hdc in next 6 sts; rep from * 7 more times (64 hdc).

Rnds 9–17: Hdc in each st around (64 hdc).

Rnd 18: *Hdc-dec, hdc in next 6 sts; rep from * 7 more times (56 hdc).

Rnd 19: *Hdc-dec, hdc in next 5 sts; rep from * 7 more times (48 hdc).

Rnd 20: *Hdc-inc, hdc in next 5 sts; rep from * 7 more times (56 hdc).

Rnds 21–26: Hdc in each st around (56 hdc).

Sc in next st, sl st in next st to finish off. Fasten off, and weave in ends.

MAKE THE EYES

Note: Each eye is worked in a spiral, so joining rounds is not necessary. Mark beginning of each round.

FIRST EYE

Rnd 1: With 2 strands of yarn held together, ch 2, sc 6 times in beg ch (6 sc).

Rnd 2: *Sc 2 times in each st; rep from * 5 more times (12 sc).

Rnd 3: *Dc 2 times in each st; rep from * 11 more times (24 sc).

Rnd 4: *Dc 2 times in next st, dc; rep from * 5 more times, tr, dtr, picot; fasten off.

SECOND EYE

Rnds 1–3: Rep First Eye instructions.

Rnd 4: Picot, dtr, tr, *dc, dc 2 times in next st; rep from * 5 more times, hdc, sc, sl st to finish off eye; fasten off and weave in ends.

ADD EYES TO BASKET

Position the right eye on the basket at the point of the last st. Using two strands of yarn and a tapestry needle, tack down the center of the eye; using the center hole as a guide, bring the needle up through the center and then back down in the first round of stitches. Continue until center is secure.

Using two strands of yarn and the outside stitches of the eye, tack down the eye securely, leaving the picot stitches unsewn. Weave in all ends. Repeat with left eye.

ADD THE BEAK

Using two strands of yarn and long straight stitches, embroider a beak between the bottoms of the eyes.

035
cozy up with a pint

Indulge in your favorite ice cream while keeping your hands warm and toasty with a crochet sleeve for a pint-size container. The sleeve works up quickly in rows of double and half double crochet, and is a unique gift that everyone will want to dig into.

YOU WILL NEED

1 ounce worsted weight acrylic yarn: turquoise

Size I crochet hook

Blunt-end yarn needle

Gauge: 9 rows and 9 hdc = 4 inches

Notes: See #169. The cozy will fit most pint-size ice cream containers.

Finished Cozy: 3 inches tall

ABBREVIATIONS:

reverse sc = working from left to right, sc in each st

CROCHET THE COZY

Rnd 1: Ch 4 (counts as first dc and beg ch). Dc 9 more times in beg ch (10 dc). Join with sl st to first dc.

Rnd 2: Ch 3 (counts as first dc), dc in same st, 2 dc in each dc around (20 dc). Join with sl st to first dc.

Rnd 3: Ch 2 (counts as first hdc), *2 hdc in next dc, 1 hdc in next 2 dc, rep from * around, 2 hdc in last dc (28 hdc). Join with sl st to first hdc.

Rnd 4: Ch 2 (counts as first hdc), turn, hdc in FRONT LOOP of each hdc around (28 hdc). Join with sl st to first hdc.

Rnd 5: Turn, ch 2 (counts as first hdc), hdc in each hdc (28 hdc). Join with sl st to first hdc.

Rnds 6–16: Rep Rnd 5 (28 hdc).

Rnd 17: Ch 1, reverse sc in each hdc around, attach to first hdc (28 rsc). Fasten off, and weave in ends.

036
fashion fingerless gloves

It can be tricky to keep your hands toasty while trying to get things done (or use your phone!), so these custom-made fingerless gloves are a clever solution. The construction uses basic crochet stitches, but you can personalize them for yourself or a friend depending on which yarn you choose. Bonus: They're perfect for wearing inside in drafty rooms during the winter.

YOU WILL NEED

Worsted weight yarn

Size I crochet hook

Tapestry needle

Notes: Gauge is not critical to the success of this project. See #169. Make two gloves, following instructions for Left and Right Hand.

CROCHET THE GLOVES

Rnd 1: Ch 25, sl st to 1st ch to make circle, being careful not to twist chain.

Rnd 2:. Rnd 1: Ch 1, hdc in same ch as join and in each st around. Sl st to top of 1st hdc (25 hdc).

Rnd 3: Rnd 2: Ch 1, hdc in same ch as join. Hdc tbl (through backloop) of each st around. Sl st to top of 1st hdc (25 hdc).

Rnds 4–12: Rep Rnd 2 (25 hdc per rnd).

Left Hand Rnd 13: (Make hole for thumb): Ch 1, hdc in same st as join. Hdc tbl of next 3 sts. Ch 4; skip next 4 sts; hdc tbl of rem sts. Sl st to top of 1st hdc (21 hdc) (4 ch).

Right Hand Rnd 14: (Make hole for thumb): Ch 1, hdc in same st as join. Hdc tbl of next 18 sts. Ch 4; sk next 4

sts; hdc tbl of rem sts. Sl sts to top of 1st hdc (21 hdc) (4 ch).

Left Hand Rnd 14: Ch 1, hdc in same st as join. Hdc tbl of next 3 sts; hdc in next 4 chs; hdc tbl of each st around. Sl st to top of 1st hdc (25 hdc).

Right Hand Rnd 14: Ch 1, hdc in same st as join. Hdc tbl of next 18 sts;

hdc in next 4 chs; hdc tbl of rem sts around. Sl st to top of 1st hdc (25 hdc).

Rnds 15–19: Rep Rnd 2. Fasten off and weave in ends (25 hdc per rnd).

037
finger-knit a cowl

Make this chunky, big-stitch cowl with just two balls of yarn and the power of your own arms! Follow our tutorial to share the warmth.

YOU WILL NEED

2 balls bulky yarn

Scissors

CAST ON

1. Hold yarn tails from both yarn balls together in one hand. Pull yarn tails to arm's length. Repeat five times to create a doubled tail five times the length of your arm (A).

2. To create a slipknot, use your right hand to wrap the doubled yarn tail clockwise around index and middle fingers of the left hand (B), then drop the doubled yarn tail behind the two fingers; pull doubled yarn tail through the circle, forming a loop (C).

3. Place the loop over your right wrist and gently tug on doubled working yarn to shape the knot. Adjust loop so it is loose on the wrist (D).

4. Wrap working yarn around left thumb, working yarn coming off front of thumb. Hold working yarn in palm with fourth and fifth fingers (E).

5. Hold yarn tails with left fingers. Slide right hand under yarn coming off front of thumb in left hand (F).

6. Hold open new loop on right wrist using your left thumb while continuing to hold yarn tails with left hand fingers (G).

7. Grab yarn tail with right hand (H) and pull between loops on right hand (I). Pull working yarn to adjust loop loosely on wrist (J).

8. Repeat Steps 5–7 ten times to complete cast-on row (K).

KNIT

1. Wrap working yarn around thumb on cast-on right arm and across palm (L).

2. While holding working yarn taut between right thumb and palm, use left hand to lift first stitch on right arm up and over loop around thumb (M).

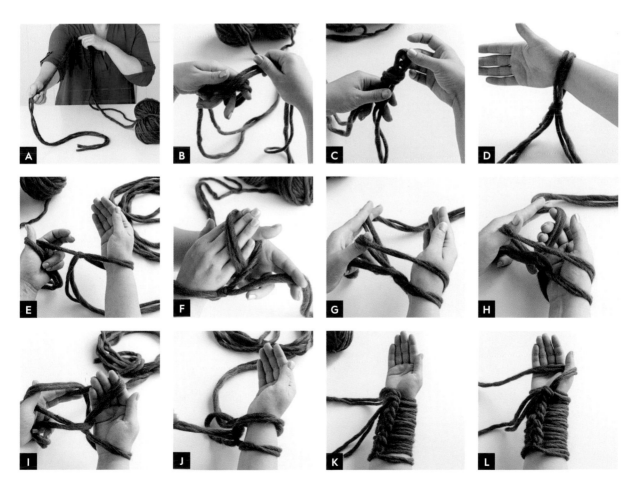

3. Insert left hand through loop (N). Adjust tension of loop on left arm. First knitted stitch is complete (O).

4. Continue to knit all stitches from right arm to left arm; first knit row is complete.

5. Repeat Step 4 to knit in opposite direction, and knit the stitches from the left arm to the right arm. Continue to knit 22 rows total (P).

CAST OFF

1. Knit two stitches (Q).

2. Hold working yarn in right hand. Pull first stitch over second stitch with left hand and tighten the loop (R).

3. Drop loop. Pull working yarn and adjust yarn on wrist.

4. Repeat Steps 1–3 until one stitch is left on wrist (S).

FINISHING

1. Cut yarn at least 6 inches longer than the width of the cowl. Make a slipknot as big as the width of the

cowl in the last loop (T).

2. Fold cowl in half with right sides together and short edges aligned. Hold yarn tails together and tuck the tails between the stitches (U).

3. Weave yarn tails in and out between the stitches, under the cast-off edge. Backstitch one or two stitches to secure the yarn. Weave in the yarn ends. Turn the cowl right side out (V).

4. Seam the ends of flat knitted piece together to make looped scarf (W).

038

quick-crochet a button scarf

Everyone will love the go-with-everything style of this button scarf. By crocheting with four strands of yarn at once, you quickly give shape to the scarf in just eight rows.

YOU WILL NEED

2—5-ounce skeins worsted weight yarn: dark green (such as Caron Simply Soft in Forest Floor)

Size P crochet hook or size needed to obtain gauge

2—1- to 1¼-inch-diameter buttons

Blunt-end yarn needle

Gauge: 7 sts and 4 rows = 4 inches in dc

Note: See #169.

Finished Size: 7½×35 inches

CROCHET THE SCARF

Note: Use both ends of each skein of yarn to work with four strands throughout the pattern.

Ch 63.

Row 1: Dc in 3rd ch from hook (counts as dc), dc in each ch (60 dc); ch 3, turn.

Row 2: Dc in each dc (60 dc); ch 3, turn.

Rows 3–8: Rep Row 2.

Fasten off and weave in ends. Sew buttons through both layers where desired.

4 Ways to Gift a White Bowl

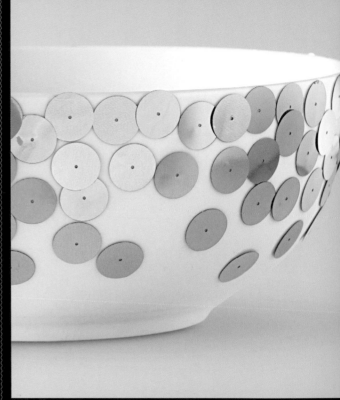

039
wrap with rope
Utility rope gives a nautical feel to a catchall. Starting at the bottom, apply a ring of hot glue and wrap chunky rope around the sides of the bowl, adding glue as you wrap.

040
adorn with sequins
Large gold sequins add festive flair at parties. Coat the outside of the bowl with decoupage medium, then stick large sequins on the bowl as desired; let dry four hours.

041
say it with clay

White clay accents offer subtle dimension. Cut leaf shapes from oven-bake clay using a crafts knife. Mold each shape around the wall of an oven-safe bowl until they stick, then bake according to package instructions. Let stand for one day before using.

042
add a little gold leaf

A golden center makes everyday items shine. Coat the interior of the bowl with two coats of gold paint. We used Martha Stewart Crafts Liquid Gilding in Gold. Use the bowl for decorative purposes only.

043
join the band

Pretty scallops, crocheted on opposite sides of a foundation chain, create a feminine headband with a curvy shape. Make it completely adjustable (and pinch-free!) with slip-stitch ties that fasten to the ends.

YOU WILL NEED

Medium weight yarn in desired color
Size G/6 (4 mm) crochet hook
Blunt-end yarn needle

Note: Gauge is not critical to the success of this project. See #169.

CROCHET THE HEADBAND

Ch 57.

Row 1: 4 dc in 3rd ch from hook, sk 2 sts, *sc in next st, sk 2 sts, 5 dc in next st, sk 2 sts * 8 times, sc in next st, sk 2 sts, 10 dc in last st.

Note: The following row is worked on the opposite side of the foundation ch.

Row 2: Sk 2 sts, * sc in next st, sk 2 sts, 5 dc in next st, sk 2 sts * 8 times, sc in next sc, sk 2 sts, 5 dc in next st. Sl st to top of first dc. Fasten off.

ADD THE TIES

Ch 21.

Row 1: Sl st in 2nd ch from hook and each st across (20 sl sts).

Use yarn needle to attach a tie to each end of the headband and weave in ends.

044

string together flowers

Perk up the edge of a shelf with a simple crochet-flower garland. Make each lacy flower using cotton yarn in bright colors, then join the flowers to a simple chain-stitched chain.

YOU WILL NEED

Worsted weight yarn (such as Lily Sugar'n Cream 100% cotton): Soft Ecru, Hot Green, Tangerine

Size H crochet hook

Tapestry needle

Note: See #169.

FLOWER

Ch 4, sl st to 1st ch to make a ring.

Rnd 1: Ch 3 (counts as 1 dc), 13 dc in ring. Join with sl st to beg ch 3 (14 dc).

Rnd 2: *Ch 3, sk next st, sl st into next st. Rep from *six more times until you reach the beg. Join with sl st to beg ch 3.

Note: You should have seven loops around your work.

Rnd 3: (Petals) In each ch 3 sp, work the following sts: sc, hdc, 2 dc, hdc, sc. Continue around flower. Sl st to first sc. You should have seven petals. Fasten off and weave in ends.

Rep to make flowers in other colors.

GARLAND

* Ch 25. Join flower to ch. Rep from *, adding flowers until desired garland length is reached.

045

make beautiful baskets

Stash yarn in a slouchy crocheted basket.

YOU WILL NEED
Size L crochet hook
T-shirt yarn

Double your yarn for a sturdier weave. Referring to #169, and the complete pattern below, single crochet in the round. When the circle is the desired size for the bottom of your basket, single crochet under the line or ridge on the back of the first stitch of previous round. Once you complete that round, continue single crocheting around the circle until the basket reaches desired height.

Ch 6, join with a sl st to create a loop. Work the first round in the loop.

Rnd 1: 8 sc in loop. Join with sl st.

Rnd 2: 2 sc in each st. Join with sl st. (16 sc)

Rnd 3: Ch 1, sc in same st, sc in next st, (2 sc in next st, sc in next st) around. Join with sl st. (24 sc)

Rnd 4: Ch 1, sc in same st, sc in next 2 sts, (2 sc in next st, sc in next 2 sts) around. Join with sl st. (32 sc)

Rnd 5: Ch 1, sc in same st, sc in next 3 sts, (2 sc in next st, sc in next 3 sts) around. Join with sl st. (40 sc)

Rnd 6: Ch 1, sc in same st, sc in next 4 sts, (2 sc in next st, sc in next 4 sts) around. Join with sl st. (48 sc) Circle should be roughly 10 inches wide now.

Continue increasing until basket is desired width, then start the first row of the body of the basket.

1st round of sides: Ch 1, sc around in front loops only. Join with sl st.

2nd round of sides: Ch 1, sc around in both loops. Join with sl st.

Repeat 2nd round of sides until your basket reaches the desired height.

046
charm your friends

There's nothing "granny" about this fresh, fun pendant except for the crocheted square at its center.

YOU WILL NEED

Embroidery floss: one skein each of three colors

Size 6 (1.8 mm) steel crochet hook

1-inch-square bezel pendant

Industrial glue (such as E-6000)

Ball chain

Note: Gauge is not critical to the success of this project. See #169.

CROCHET THE GRANNY SQUARE

Row 1: Ch 3 (counts as 1st hdc), 11 hdc in 3rd ch from hook, join with sl st to top of beg ch 3 (12 hdc). Fasten off.

Rnd 2: With new color and using a sl st, join to any hdc. Ch 3, sc in same st. 1 sc in each of next 2 hdc. *(sc, ch2, sc) in next st, 1 sc in each of next 2 hdc, repeat from * twice more. Join with sl st to 1st ch of beg ch 3. Fasten off.

Rnd 3: With new color and using a sl st, join to any ch 2 sp. Ch 3, sc in same st. 1 sc in each of next 4 sc. *(sc, ch 2, sc) in next ch 2 sp, 1 sc in each of next 4 sc, repeat from * twice more. Join with sl st to 1st ch of beg ch 3. Fasten off.

FINISH THE NECKLACE

Tighten center circle and weave in loose ends. Spread a small amount of glue inside the square bezel and position crocheted granny square inside. Cut ball chain to desired length and thread bezel pendant onto chain.

047

incite a chain reaction

This crocheted chain is the ultimate in versatility. Wrap it around your wrist for a fashionable stacked bracelet, or drape the strand around your neck.

YOU WILL NEED
Sport weight yarn
Size E/4 (3.5 mm) crochet hook
¼-inch-diameter button

Note: Gauge is not critical to the success of this project. See #169.

1. Make a chain approximately 72 inches long. Sl st in 6th ch from hook (buttonhole made) and in each ch across.

2. Attach button to beg of ch using tails. Fasten off and weave in ends.

048

go beyond bangles

A crocheted cuff is pretty, versatile, and comfy too! This lacy band is crocheted using perle cotton for a soft flexible fit and fastens with two small buttons inserted into the crochet holes on the ends.

YOU WILL NEED

DMC perle cotton, size 3: ecru
Size 2 (2.25 mm) steel crochet hook
2—¼-inch-diameter buttons

Note: Gauge is not critical to the success of this project. See #169.

Ch 8.

Row 1: Sc in 2nd ch from hook and in each ch across, turn.

Row 2: Ch 3 (counts as 1st dc), dc in next st, sk 1 st, 5 dc in next st, sk 1 st, dc in last 2 sts, turn.

Row 3: Ch 3, dc in next st, ch 1, sk 2 sts, (dc, ch 1, dc) in next st, ch 1, sk 2 sts, dc in last 2 sts, turn.

Row 4: Ch 3, dc in next st, sk ch 1 and next st, 5 dc in next ch 1 sp, sk next st and ch 1 sp, dc in last 2 dc, turn.

Rows 5–22: Rep rows 3 and 4.

Row 23: Ch 1, sc in 1st 2 sts, ch 2, sk next st, sc in next 3 sts, ch 2, sk next st, sc in last 2 sts.

Fasten off and weave in ends. Sew on buttons.

049
bring your own bag

The handle openings are formed by skipping stitches as you crochet the rows. Fold the panel in half and stitch the sides together to complete the clutch.

YOU WILL NEED

Worsted weight yarn

Size H/8 (5 mm) crochet hook

Clear plastic makeup or toiletries bag for liner (clutch shown uses an 11×6-inch bag)

Approximately 15-inch square of printed fabric

Sewing thread

Blunt-end yard needle

Cardboard

Tulle

Felt

Small beads

Pin back

Finished Clutch: Approximately 12×9 inches

Gauge: 7 sts and 6 rows = 2 inch. Take time to check your gauge.

Note: See #169.

CROCHET THE CLUTCH

Ch 45.

Row 1: Hdc in 3rd ch from hook, 42 hdc, turn (44 sts).

Rows 2–5: Ch 2, hdc in next st, 42 hdc, turn.

Row 6: Ch 2, hdc in next st, 12 hdc, ch 16, sk the next 16 hdc, hdc in next 14 sts, turn (this creates one handle).

Row 7: Ch 2, hdc in next st, 12 hdc, 16 hdc in next 16 ch, hdc in next 14 sts, turn.

Rows 8–39: Ch 2, hdc in next st, 42

hdc, turn. **Note:** The number of crochet rows needed depends on how tall your cosmetic bag liner is. If needed, adjust the number of crochet rows to make your bag one row higher than the height of the zipped liner.

Rows 40–41: Rep Rows 6–7 (this creates second handle).

Rows 42–45: Ch 2, hdc in next st, 42 hdc. Fasten off. Weave in ends.

ADD LINING AND FINISH CLUTCH

1. Lay the crocheted fabric flat. Measure width and distance from just below one handle to just below the other handle. Cut fabric 1 inch wider and taller than measurements.

2. Fold ½ inch hem on all sides of fabric; press. Lay fabric right side up on inside of crocheted fabric. Slip-stitch the fabric to crocheted fabric with matching thread.

3. Fold crocheted fabric in half with

lining on the inside. Align the handles. Use yarn and a blunt-end yarn needle to whipstitch the sides of the clutch together. Tie off yarn and trim the ends.

4. Insert cosmetic bag liner inside crocheted clutch, leaving zipper open. Hand-stitch the liner to the crocheted clutch (along the zipper binding) using matching thread.

MAKE FLOWER PIN

1. Cut a small flower shape from cardboard. Using cardboard flower as a template, trace onto tulle three times; cut out.

2. Cut small circle from felt for backing. Layer the tulle shapes on top of the felt circle, alternating the position of the petals. Sew in place at center. Stitch three or four beads to the center of the tulle flower.

3. Sew pin back to the back of felt circle. Pin flower to crocheted clutch.

050
add flair with trims

Take your crochet skills over the edge with colorful trims. Add edgings to pillowcases (shown here), tea towels, skirts, or wherever you want a bit of eye-catching detail.

YOU WILL NEED
Pillowcases
Water-soluble marking pen
Large-eye embroidery needle
Sport weight/DK cotton yarn in desired color
Size E/4 (3.5 mm) crochet hook

Note: Gauge is not crucial to the success of this project. See #169.

1. Turn pillowcase inside out. Beginning ¼ inch from pillowcase edge, use a water-soluble marking pen to mark dots every ½ inch along the inside of pillowcase band (A).

2. Foundation Rnd: Measure a length of yarn 15 times the width of the pillowcase opening. Fold the yarn in half and knot the ends.

3. Working from inside pillowcase band, blanket-stitch the edge. To blanket stitch, refer to photos and diagram, opposite.

4. Push needle through a marked dot to outside of pillowcase. Form a reverse L shape with the yarn, and hold angle of L shape in place with your thumb. Push the needle down into next dot to the right. Come up under the reverse L shape and, crossing over the trailing thread to secure the stitch, again form a reverse L shape with the yarn. Push the needle down at the next marked dot to the right and come up under the reverse L shape (B). Continue around pillowcase band.

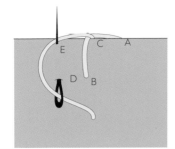

BLANKET-STITCH DIAGRAM

5. To join end of blanket stitches to beginning, bring needle through front of first stitch knot (C). Tie off.

6. Turn pillowcase right side out. Make a slip knot on crochet hook and insert hook under blanket stitch (D). **Note:** The first stitch can begin anywhere.

BEGIN EDGING (for all edgings)

Rnd 1: 3 sc in each st (E), join to first sc with sl st.

PILLOWCASE #1 (yellow case with green edging)

Rnd 2: Ch 4, dc in same st, * sk next 2 sc, (dc, ch 1, dc) in next st. Rep from * to end. Sl st to 3rd ch of beg ch 4.

Rnd 3: * (sc, ch 3, sc) in next ch 1 sp, sk next 2 dc. Rep from * to end. Sl st to 1st sc. Fasten off.

PILLOWCASE #2 (green case with cream edging)

Rnd 2: Ch 5, sk next 2 sc; * dc in next sc, ch 2, sk next 2 sc. Rep from * to end. Sl st to 3rd ch of beg ch 5.

Rnd 3: Ch 1, * 3 sc in next ch 2 sp, ch 1, sk next dc. Rep from * to end. Sl st to beg ch 1. Fasten off.

PILLOWCASE #3 (blue case with orange edging)

Rnd 2: *Ch 1, sk 2 sc, (2 dc, ch 1, 2 dc) in next sc, ch 1, sk 2 sc, sl st in next sc. Rep from * to end. Sl st to 1st sc. Fasten off.

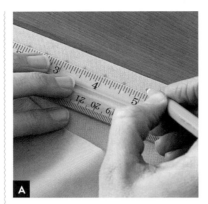

A

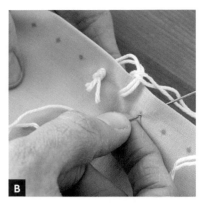

B

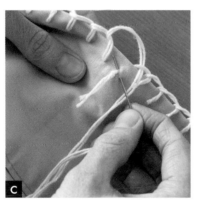

C

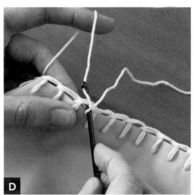

D

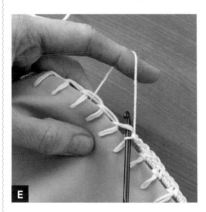

E

051
tie up a trivet

Protect your tabletop from steaming cookware with a chunky knotted trivet. Be sure to select rope made from all-natural fibers that won't melt with heat.

YOU WILL NEED

½-inch cotton rope (we used about 14 feet)

Duct tape

Hot-glue gun and glue sticks

Finished Trivet: 8 inches across

1. Wrap duct tape around ends of cotton rope to prevent fraying. Form a pretzel shape with the long end of the rope trailing on the right-hand side (A).

2. Bring the short end of the rope over long end and under the first loop (B).

3. Continue weaving over and under each section (C).

4. Bring the long end around to the left and follow the path created with the short end, weaving over and under each section (D).

5. Pull through to create a fourth loop at the bottom (E).

6. Continue weaving the long end, following the same path around the four sides of the trivet (F).

7. Tighten loops as you go around, a total of three times (G). Hot-glue the ends on the back (H).

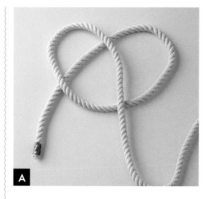

052
polish a pillow

Leave the tails of a double infinity knot long, and the result is an interesting wrap for a purchased pillow.

YOU WILL NEED
Rope, yarn, or cording
Purchased pillow

1. Depending on the size of your pillow, cut an even number of long lengths of rope, yarn, or cording, and separate into two groups. Shape one group into a flat loop as shown (A).

2. Lace the second group through the tails of the first loop, following the arrows as shown (B).

3. Cross the tails of the second group, following the arrows and noting how the tails overlap. The tails should be on top of the loops (C).

4. Tuck two opposite tails through the loops. Leave two remaining tails on top of the loops (D).

5. Gently pull the tails to tighten the knot, adjusting the yarn as needed to keep the knot flat (E).

6. Tie the ends together on the back of the pillow.

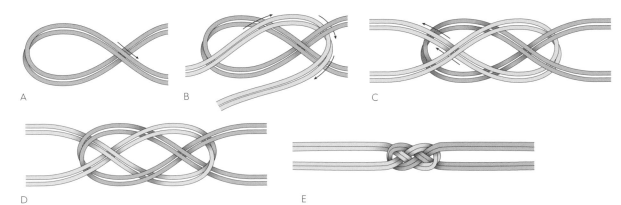

A

B

C

D

E

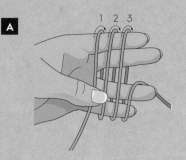
A

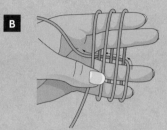
B

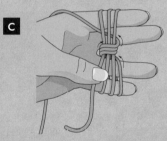
C

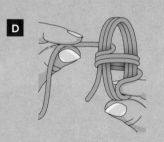
D

053

key in to creativity

Once you get the basic knot-tying technique down, you'll be making and giving them by the dozen.

YOU WILL NEED (for one keychain)

Approximately 1 yard of paracord (length will vary based on size of marble and thickness of paracord)

Glass marble

1¼-inch-diameter split key ring

Lighter

1. To make Monkey's Fist Knot: With an 8-inch tail in palm of hand, wrap rope up and over fingers three times (A).

2. Tuck working end outside the loops at back of hand, pulling end to palm side through middle of fingers as shown (B).

3. Wrap working end around both back and palm loops two times (C).

4. On third pass, wrap working end around palm loops only and exit through center to side with tail (D).

5. Bring the working end through hole below center loops and wrap up and over loops three times, securing the core. Exit working yarn through the center to side with tail (E).

6. Insert marble into center of knot. Adjust loops on each side of knot to tighten the knot around the core (F).

7. Cut both tails to about 8 inches. Wrap each side of knot three times.

8. Bring beginning and end tail together, and tie an overhand knot around the key ring about 2 inches from the Monkey's Fist Knot.

9. Cut the excess paracord from the tails, close to the overhand knot. Using a lighter, carefully melt the ends of the paracord to secure the knot and prevent unraveling.

10. Add key ring to one looped end.

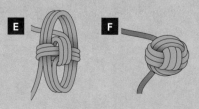
E   **F**

twist a chew toy

Give a canine friend a treat with a sisal rope monkey's fist knot wrapped around a tennis ball core. A loop makes throwing the toy and playing tug even more fun.

YOU WILL NEED

Tennis ball

25 feet of medium weight sisal rope

Duct tape

Finished Toy: 5 inches round (without loop)

1. Wrap the ends of the sisal rope with duct tape to prevent fraying.

2. Following knot-tying instructions in #053, make a monkey's fist knot around the tennis ball using the rope. Wrap each portion of the knot four times. Adjust the wraps so they are slightly loose around ball.

3. Cut the rope tail to 16 inches long; wrap the cut end with duct tape. Bend the tail in half and insert the duct-tape end underneath the wraps beside the beginning of the tail to make a loop. Adjust the wraps to tighten the knot around the ball and to hold the tail securely.

055
knot a bracelet

Two colors of cording give a double infinity knot a fashionable look as a bracelet. Glue the cord ends into metal end caps found in the jewelry-making aisle at the crafts store, and add a lobster clasp.

YOU WILL NEED

9 feet each of cording in two contrasting colors

Crafts glue

2—10-millimeter metal end caps

2 jump rings

Jewelry pliers

Lobster clasp

1. Cut four 24-inch cording lengths from each color.

2. Following knot-tying instructions in #052, make a double infinity knot using two groups of four cording lengths each.

3. Fit knot around wrist. Trim tails to desired length.

4. Insert glue inside a metal end cap then insert all four cording tails from one side of the bracelet into the cap. Repeat on other side. Let dry.

5. Using jewelry pliers, attach a jump ring to the loop on each metal end cap. Attach lobster clasp to each jump ring.

Embroidery

Transform simple stitches into delightful gifts to wear, use, and display—whether for big occasions, special holidays, or just because.

056

stitch on scarves

A strip of cotton becomes a one-of-a-kind scarf with designs using simple stitches.

YOU WILL NEED
Cotton fabric
Scissors
Water-soluble marking pen
Embroidery floss
Large-eye embroidery needle
Sewing pins

1. Cut cotton fabric to desired scarf length.

2. For eyelets, draw circles with fabric pen. Thread needle and insert needle on the backside of fabric on the circle, then make parallel whipstitches around the circle, looping needle over thread between each stitch. Repeat, using different colors as desired, in a heart shape or scattered randomly.

3. For fabric stripes, secure strips of cotton to scarf with pins, then whipstitch to create perfectly imperfect stripes. (See #168.)

057
string on sparkles

Turn ordinary cardstock into personalized notes. Prepunch holes around the edge of a card, then run thread through the diamond pattern, attaching bugle beads along the way.

YOU WILL NEED

Cardstock

Cardboard

T-pln

Button/crafts thread

Needles, small and large

Bugle beads (or desired beads)

Scissors

1. Place cardboard under cardstock, then use a T-pin to poke holes in a diamond pattern around the edges of the card. (Each diamond side should be a bit longer than a bead.) Put the cardboard aside while you stitch the beads to the card stock.

2. Cut 2 long strands of thread.

3. Single-thread both strands of thread through the larger needle. Knot together one end of the strands. Pull the two strands through from front to back, so that the knot is at the front of the work, and the two free strands are at the back.

4. Switch to a small needle that will fit a bead over the eye and single-thread one strand of thread into the eye. Backstitch up through the

next hole (see #168), thread a bead, and stitch back through first hole.

5. Continue this pattern (stitching up through the next hole, threading a bead, and stitching back through the previous hole) along one side of the diamond pattern.

6. Once finished with one side, remove the needle, let the thread of the finished strand hang, and thread the second strand. Continue pattern to meet the first strand. Knot together and trim excess thread. Continue around the border of the card.

058
feather a nest

Make a custom piece of art with a series of nature-inspired stitches.

YOU WILL NEED

14×16-inch piece of gray linen

Water-soluble marking pen

Embroidery hoop

Embroidery floss: navy blue, dark coral, light coral, white, yellow, light blue

Embroidery needle

Foam-core board

Tape

8×10-inch picture frame

Light blue acrylic paint

Foam paintbrush

1. Enlarge the feather pattern on Pattern Page F to desired size. Using a light box or sunny window, trace the pattern onto gray linen using a water-soluble marking pen.

2. Place linen in embroidery hoop and pull taut.

3. Use six strands of embroidery floss for all stitches. Refer to #168.

4. Remove fabric from hoop. Dab the fabric with warm water and a clean cloth to erase the tracing lines. Using a warm iron and working on wrong side, press the finished embroidery.

5. Cut foam-core board to fit opening of picture frame. Mount the fabric to the board. For best results, trim fabric 2 inches beyond foam-core board, fold it around board, and tape in place, starting in center of each edge and working outward.

6. Paint picture frame with light blue acrylic paint; let dry. Insert embroidery in picture frame.

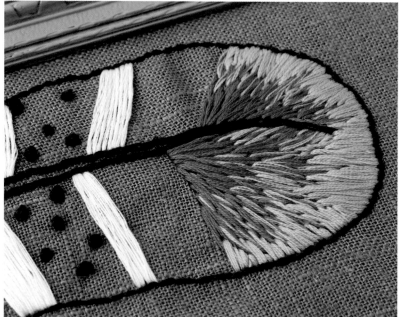

059

embroider
fanciful florals

This pretty table covering will enliven every dining nook, no matter what's on the menu.

YOU WILL NEED
Tablecloth
Air-soluble marking pen
Embroidery hoop
Embroidery floss
Embroidery needle

Mark a few wavy lines in a rambling, natural design. Add simple leaf and flower shapes, then working with an embroidery hoop, cover the pen lines with a running stitch of embroidery floss. Embellish just a corner or go bold with a larger design.

060
bring in the outdoors

Create an embroidery hoop duo featuring lavender stalks and a wispy crop of dandelions.

YOU WILL NEED (for each design)

16-inch square of linen

Water-soluble marking pen

7-inch- and 10-inch-diameter wooden embroidery hoops

Perle cotton and embroidery floss for desired project*

Tapestry needle

1. Using a water-soluble marking pen, trace desired pattern on Pattern Page E, onto center of linen square. Center linen in 10-inch-diameter embroidery hoop. Pull fabric taut; tighten screw.

2. Following the pattern and color key, stitch the design using three strands of embroidery floss for French knots flowers and perle cotton for stem-stitched stems. To stitch French knots and to stem-stitch, see #168.

3. Remove fabric from hoop. Using a warm iron and working on wrong side, press finished embroidery. Insert fabric into 7-inch-diameter wooden embroidery hoop, centering design and pulling fabric taut; tighten screw. Finish back of embroidery following instructions in #168.

*For dandelion design: Size 5 perle cotton #3348 celery green; DMC embroidery floss #3348 celery green and #758 dusty pink.

*For lavender design: Size 5 perle cotton #3348 celery green; DMC embroidery floss #3042 light purple and #3041 medium purple.

061
give the key to your heart

Create a piece of cross-stitch embroidery-hoop art featuring old-fashioned keys to mark the spot where the modern ones hang.

YOU WILL NEED

10-inch square of 14-count Aida cloth

6-inch-diameter wooden embroidery hoop

DMC embroidery floss: #472, #606, #964

Size 24 tapestry needle

Note: Pattern is on Pattern Page G.

1. Place Aida cloth in embroidery hoop if desired, centering the fabric. Pull fabric taut; tighten screw.

2. Following the chart and color key on Pattern Page G, center and cross-stitch the design using three strands of embroidery floss over one square of the fabric. To cross-stitch, see #168.

3. Remove fabric from embroidery hoop. Using a warm iron and working on wrong side, press finished embroidery. Insert fabric into hoop, centering the design and pulling fabric taut. Finish back of embroidery following instructions in #168.

4 Ways to Gift Embroidery Hoops

062
plant a felt forest

Trace patterns on Pattern Page C and cut out pieces as shown in the photo above onto felt. Center a patterned fabric square in embroidery hoop, pulling taut. Tighten the screw. Refer to the pattern for placement, and position felt trees and leaves on the fabric. Pin to hold the pieces in place. Use one strand of matching embroidery floss to blanket-stitch the tree edges. Use small tack stitches to secure the leaf edges. Remove the embroidery from the hoop and press with a warm iron on the wrong side if needed. Reinsert the design into the hoop. Finish back of embroidery following instructions in #168.

063
pick a dandelion

Trace the pattern on Pattern Page B on the right side of cotton fabric. Center design and pull fabric taut in an embroidery hoop. Tighten the screw. Use four strands of floss to chain-stitch the dandelion stem. Use two strands of embroidery floss and a long straight stitch for each dandelion pouf line. Add a double-wrapped French knot at the end of each long stitch. Use one strand of embroidery floss to fly-stitch floating florets (fly stitching tutorials are available online). Remove from hoop and press on the wrong side. Reinsert into the hoop. Finish back of embroidery following instructions in #168.

064
get the scoop on hoops

Fill a range of sizes of embroidery hoops with pretty
fabrics, trimming just to fit after screwing tightly and
pulling taut. Make an assortment of coordinating
pieces to gift a set. Layer on concentric circles of
smaller hoops by cutting a piece of batting to fit under
the smaller circle. Tack-stitch a button in the center
through all layers to secure in place. Finish back of hoop
following instructions in #168.

065
tell the time

Fill a 10-inch embroidery hoop with a 16-inch square of
white linen fabric. Trace the pattern on Pattern Pages
J and K onto the linen, marking a small dot at center.
Do not trace the outer edge of the pattern. Reposition
the linen in the embroidery hoop, centering the design
inside the opening. Use three strands of embroidery floss
for all stitches. Backstitch all numeral outlines in colors
listed on key found with pattern. Fill numerals with stitches
indicated. Fill back with a circle of foam core, and use a

066

make linens lovely

Whether you need a gift for a foodie or for someone who simply likes to eat, these embroidered linens and framed artwork add whimsy and fun to any kitchen.

YOU WILL NEED

2 linen hand towels

Rickrack: 1-inch-wide orange, ¼-inch-wide orange, ½-inch-wide teal

¾-inch-wide twill tape: teal

Sewing thread: teal and orange

Sewing needle

18-inch square of teal wool

Transfer paper

Stylus or dried-up ballpoint pen

Embroidery hoop

Perle cotton: Valdani size 12 #0/244 (variegated orange), Valdani size 12 #0/550 (variegated teal), and DMC size 5 Ecru

Embroidery needle

Square frame with 1½-inch-square opening

1. Measure width of towel and cut rickrack and twill tape ½ inch longer than measurement. Referring to photo for placement, hand-sew rickrack and twill tape to the hemmed edge of the towel using matching sewing thread and tiny tack stitches. Tuck under the rickrack raw ends and stitch in place.

2. Use a light box or sunny window to trace whisk and cutlery patterns on Pattern Page H onto hand towels using a sharp pencil. Position the whisk approximately ½ inch above the rickrack and the cutlery 1½ inches above the rickrack. For the framed piece, trace the pattern on Pattern

Page H. Lay transfer paper onto teal wool. Lay mixing bowl and mixer pattern on transfer paper. Using a stylus or dried-up ballpoint pen, carefully and firmly trace design to transfer onto wool.

3. Place towel or wool in embroidery hoop. Referring to color key on patterns for thread colors and stitches, embroider the designs.

4. Remove the embroidery from hoop. Using a warm iron, press the finished embroidery.

5. For the framed piece, hand-stitch ¼-inch-wide orange rickrack to the mixer as shown in the photo, using matching sewing thread and tiny tack stitches. Tuck under the raw ends before securing. Insert embroidery into frame.

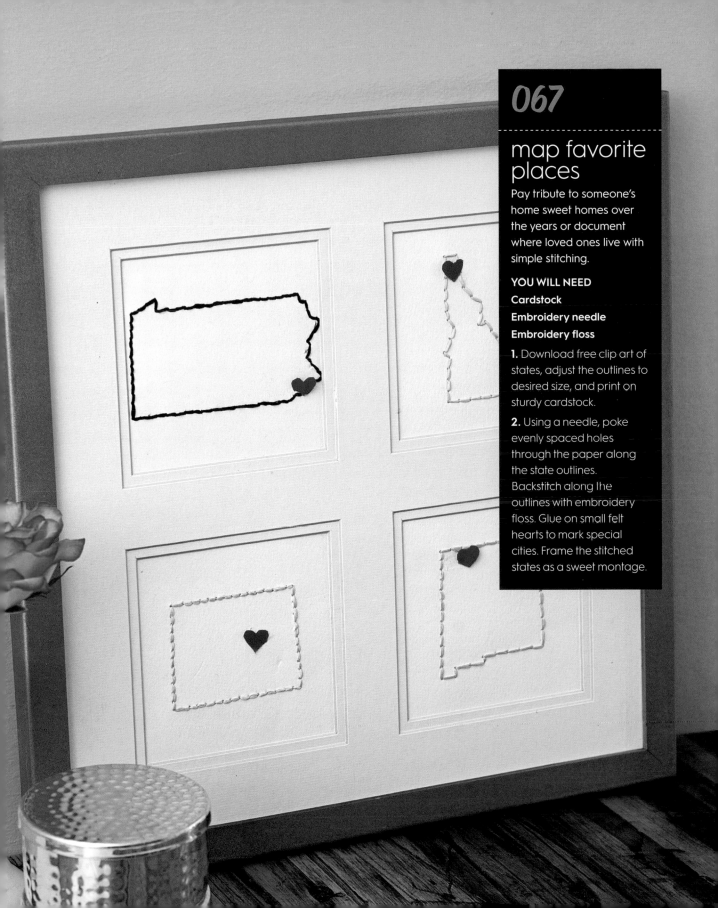

map favorite places

Pay tribute to someone's home sweet homes over the years or document where loved ones live with simple stitching.

YOU WILL NEED

Cardstock

Embroidery needle

Embroidery floss

1. Download free clip art of states, adjust the outlines to desired size, and print on sturdy cardstock.

2. Using a needle, poke evenly spaced holes through the paper along the state outlines. Backstitch along the outlines with embroidery floss. Glue on small felt hearts to mark special cities. Frame the stitched states as a sweet montage.

068

bring blossoms to a band

Dainty and simple in lazy daisies and cross-stitches, this felt headband attached to an elastic strap is a delightful adornment.

YOU WILL NEED

2—1×12-inch pieces of light gray felt
Water-soluble marking pen
DMC embroidery floss: #504, #842, #3024, #3778
Embroidery needle
11-inch piece of ¼-inch-wide rubberized elastic

1. Using a light box or sunny window, trace pattern on Pattern Page F onto one piece of light gray felt using a water-soluble marking pen.

2. Use three strands of embroidery floss for all stitches. For stitch diagrams and instructions, see #168.

3. Pin ends of rubberized elastic approximately 1 inch from each narrow edge of second piece of felt. Machine-sew the ends of rubberized elastic in place.

4. Place felt pieces together with wrong sides facing. Stitch the pieces together using one strand of floss and a running stitch just inside the felt edges.

069

cuff yourself with chevrons

Create a felt cuff with a chevron pattern in no time.

YOU WILL NEED

2—¾×8-inch pieces of light gray felt

Water-soluble marking pen

DMC embroidery floss: #779, #842, #3024, #3858, #3859

Embroidery needle

Black snap

1. Using a light box or sunny window, trace pattern on Pattern Page D onto one piece of light gray felt using a water-soluble marking pen.

2. Use three strands of embroidery floss for all stitches. Refer to the Lazy Daisy Stitch Diagram, below, to stitch the design. For more details, see #168.

3. Place felt pieces together with wrong sides facing. Stitch the pieces together using one strand of embroidery floss and a running stitch just inside the felt edges.

4. Referring to the pattern for placement, center and hand-stitch one half of the snap to one end of the embroidered piece end. Bring the opposite end around to match up the bracelet ends. Mark the placement of the remaining snap half; hand-sew the snap half in place.

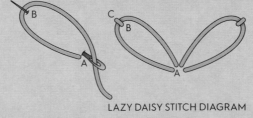

LAZY DAISY STITCH DIAGRAM

Clay, Glass & Resin

With texture, reflective qualities, and endless ways to add variety, you'll want to try your hand at these craft projects—even if the materials are new to you.

070
play with clay

Who doesn't need a pretty little dish to hold small items? Roll out white polymer clay, then add textural details with a variety of objects, such as a pencil eraser, paper doilies, or rubber stamps. Trim the edges into the desired shapes before baking each dish.

YOU WILL NEED

White polymer clay

Acrylic roller

Wooden rods

Die-cut circle or heart shape

Toothpick

Items to texturize the clay: pencil eraser, rubber stamp, paper doilies

Ink pad in desired colors

Small round paper bowl

Baking sheet

Fine-grit sandpaper

Foam paintbrush

Acrylic paint

Fine-tip artist's paintbrush (optional)

Decoupage medium

1. Following manufacturer's instructions, condition the clay. Place clay on a smooth, hard surface. Using acrylic roller, roll out clay to ¼-inch thickness. To do this, position a wooden rod on each side of the clay. Place the roller across the clay and wooden rods; roll the clay to a consistent thickness (A).

2. For a circle or heart-shape dish, lay die-cut circle or heart on the flattened clay. Trace around the shape with a toothpick to cut it out (B). **Note:** The jagged edges will be sanded later.

3. Using texturizing items of your choice, stamp or emboss the clay with a pencil eraser or rubber stamp. Press eraser or rubber stamp into ink pad before pressing the design into the clay (C).

4. For lacelike embossing, place a stack of six paper doilies on the clay and roll over the doilies with the acrylic roller until an impression is made (D). Trim around the edges of the doilies with a toothpick. Carefully remove the doilies from the clay.

5. Place a small paper bowl right side down on a baking sheet. Place clay right side down on top of bowl, gently pressing the edges of the clay to round them against the curvature of the bowl.

6. Following the clay manufacturer's instructions, bake the clay. Allow the clay to cool thoroughly.

7. Sand the dish with fine-grit sandpaper; wipe off the sanding dust.

8. Using a foam paintbrush, brush the dish with acrylic paint if desired. If needed, use a fine-tip paintbrush to paint in grooves, ridges, or stamped areas; remove excess paint with paper towel. Let the paint dry.

9. Paint the dish with decoupage medium; let dry.

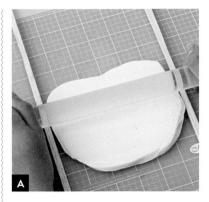

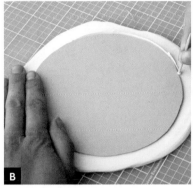

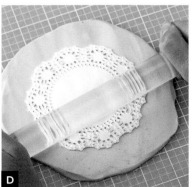

071
hang a mod planter

Balls of white polymer clay cover the surface of a hanging planter that fits any decor.

YOU WILL NEED
Oven-safe flowerpot
Parchment paper
White polymer clay
Clay roller or rolling pin
Marker
Bamboo skewer
Jute cording

1. Turn the flowerpot upside down and cover with parchment paper. Knead the clay, then roll out a thin sheet with a clay roller or rolling pin. Press the clay around the parchment paper on the pot's exterior and trim as needed.

2. Form balls and press them onto the clay sheet.

3. Press a small round object, such as a marker cap, into each ball. Using a bamboo skewer, poke three evenly spaced holes around the rim of the planter. Bake according to the manufacturer's instructions; let cool.

4. Remove the clay from the flowerpot form. Roll out another thin sheet of clay, and press it inside the clay pot to strengthen the liner. Repoke the holes, and bake again. Once cool, thread jute through the holes and tie as a hanger.

072
build a home for buds

Inside this geometric clay vase is a glass test tube, which is just the right size to hold a few flower stems.

YOU WILL NEED
Turquoise and white polymer clay
Glass test tube
Pencil
Knife

1. Knead turquoise and white polymer clays together to get the desired shade, then form the clay evenly around the test tube in a ball, making sure the tube is centered in the clay and the opening is uncovered. If needed, poke a pencil through the clay to clear the opening.

2. Slice shallow pieces of clay off the ball using a sharp knife and straight strokes to form the geometric surface. Follow the manufacturer's instructions to bake the clay; let cool.

073

say cheese

Give a cheese lover a set of custom clay cheese identifiers to dress up a cheese plate for any occasion.

YOU WILL NEED
Air-dry clay
Cookie cutters
Stamps
Bamboo skewers
Small paintbrush
Brown acrylic paint

1. Roll out a thin, even layer of air-dry clay, then cut out shapes using small cookie cutters. Stamp letters and designs onto half the shapes. You will need two shapes for each marker, one stamped and one plain.

2. Cut 4-inch-long segments from the pointed ends of bamboo skewers. Sandwich a skewer segment between the clay layers. Seal the edges with a dampened finger; let dry. Wiggle the skewer periodically as the clay dries so it is removable and replaceable.

3. Use a small brush to push brown acrylic paint into the stamped designs. Gently wipe paint from each surface with a clean cloth so the designs retain the paint; let dry.

074
mobilize clay flowers

Cookie cutters make it easy to cut clay flowers for this driftwood mobile that will be at home in a girl's room, whether she's little or grown up.

YOU WILL NEED

Pink, lavender, and white polymer clay

Clay roller or rolling pin

Cookie cutters

Lace

Bamboo skewers

Parchment paper

Driftwood

Monofilament thread or fishing line

Jute cording

1. Roll out clay to ¼-inch thickness, then use flower-shape cookie cutters to cut out flowers (A). Press pieces of lace or other items onto the surface of each flower to make patterns, poke a hole for hanging in each flower (B).

2. Place the shapes on a cookie sheet lined with parchment paper, and bake according to clay manufacturer's instructions. When cool, hang the shapes from a piece of driftwood using varying lengths of thread. Tie a thick piece of jute or rope around the center of the driftwood and hang the mobile from a ceiling hook.

075

make mercury glass

Give glass votives and shapely glass vases a makeover that sparkles and shines. The technique is easy. Just spray the inside surfaces with water; then immediately spray on mirrorlike spray paint that resembles mercury glass when dry.

YOU WILL NEED

Glass votive or vase

Spray bottle filled with water

Krylon Looking Glass Mirror-Like spray paint

Newspaper or paper plate

1. Wash glass votive or vase with soap and water; dry. Spray water on inside of glass (A).

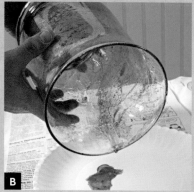

2. While wet, lightly spray inside of glass with mirror-like spray paint. Holding onto the outside of the glass, swirl the paint around the inside until the entire interior is coated (B).

3. Place glass upside down on newspaper or paper plate; let dry. Repeat process with water and paint four to five times or until satisfied with the effect (C).

076

fix up a votive with fabric

Wrap inexpensive plain glass votives in fabric to bring their beauty to light.

YOU WILL NEED
Fabric
Votive candles
Decoupage medium

Cut fabric to fit around the votive. Brush a coat of decoupage medium onto the glass, wrap with fabric, and apply another coat of the sealer. Let dry, then insert candles. Tie on a tag to finish if desired.

4 Ways to Gift a White Frame

077
fancify the corners
Tiny gold studs are the striking accents to this delicate giclée. The studs are Brass Jewel Dazzles stickers

078
add corner brackets
Gold-tone accents add a hard edge to a soft floral watercolor. Purchase four 4-inch flat corner braces

079
wrap in floral fabric

A frame wrapped in floral fabric echoes the sweet styling of a watercolor floral. Cut about 1 yard of lightweight fabric (such as cotton lawn) into 1½-inch-wide strips. Remove the glass, mat, and backing from the frame. Tape one end of a strip to the back center of the frame and begin wrapping the fabric tightly around the frame to cover. Repeat as needed with additional strips to cover the frame.

080
layer on washi tape

Strips of 1-inch-wide washi tape add an easy-to-place, removable accent in just minutes. Choose a portrait or still life with a simple background that won't compete with the patterned tape.

081
capture tiny treasures

Tiny glass bottles and vials become fascinating displays thanks to clear epoxy resin. Wire poked into the stoppers keeps objects upright.

YOU WILL NEED

Small wide-mouth glass bottle or vial with cork stopper

Object to fit inside bottle

Copper wire

Wire snips

Crafts glue

Vellum

Spray adhesive

Basic casting resin supplies (opposite)

Coarse glitter: gold

Toothpick

Note: Always work with resin in a well-ventilated area.

1. With the cork attached, measure the distance from the top of the cork to the bottom of the bottle or vial. Cut a piece of copper wire this length.

2. Remove the cork stopper, and place it bottom side up on work surface. Place a dab of glue on one end of the wire, and insert it into the center of the cork, about halfway through. Reattach the cork to the bottle to test-fit. Depending on the object you wish to mount on the wire, trim wire as needed. Glue object onto wire end. **Note:** Pay attention to direction of object on wire because it might need to be mounted upside down so it is right side up when inserted into the bottle. Adjust length of wire as needed for desired placement of the object inside bottle.

3. If desired, add vellum details such as the waves shown in the ship bottle. To make waves, cut two small rectangles from vellum to fit front and back of bottle. Trim top of each rectangle in a scallop pattern. Spray adhesive onto one side of each piece of vellum, then insert the pieces into the bottle. Use your finger to press the pieces to the front and back of bottle; let dry.

4. Follow the instructions, opposite, to prepare the resin mixture.

5. Pour resin into bottle or vial until almost full. Sprinkle a small amount of coarse gold glitter into resin if desired, and use a toothpick to swirl it into the wet resin. Replace cork on bottle while plunging the object into the wet resin. Allow to harden up to 72 hours to ensure a strong bond.

use epoxy resin

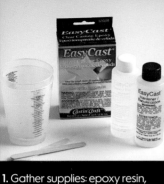

1. Gather supplies: epoxy resin, hardener, plastic measuring cups, stir sticks, and mold release spray.

2. Always work in a well-ventilated area. Pour epoxy resin into a plastic measuring cup.

3. Add an equal amount of hardener on top of the epoxy resin in the same measuring cup.

4. Stir the mixture thoroughly for two minutes, scraping the sides occasionally and being careful to avoid air bubbles by not mixing too vigorously.

5. Pour the mixture into a second clean measuring cup. Stir the mixture for one minute. If making removable resin casts, coat your mold of choice with mold release spray before pouring in resin.

6. Pour epoxy resin mixture into a mold, such as a silicone pan, a jewelry finding, or a bottle. Allow to harden up to 72 hours to ensure a strong bond. **(Note:** Use this pan only for resin, and not for food.**)**

embellish resin

1. Partially fill mold with epoxy resin. If desired, add a drop of pigment or dye, then stir with toothpick. Add glitter on top.

2. Add larger items, such as sequins, being careful not to get resin on your fingers. If needed, wear rubber gloves.

3. To prevent a heavy object from sinking too far in the resin, let the resin set up for a few minutes before dropping it in. Allow to harden up to 72 hours.

084
make memorable coasters

Custom coasters are thoughtful gifts, and the durable, high-gloss clear coat of epoxy resin is a wonderful way to enjoy photos every day.

YOU WILL NEED
Photos or handwriting samples
Laser printer
Lightweight white paper
4½-inch wood squares
Spray adhesive
Painter's tape
Basic casting resin supplies
  (see #082)
Fine-grit sandpaper

Note: Always work with resin in a well-ventilated area.

1. Print photos or handwriting samples using a laser printer onto lightweight white paper. Trim photos to 4 inches square. Trim handwriting samples to 4½ inches square.

2. Adhere a laser-print photo or handwriting sample to a wood square using spray adhesive.

3. To prevent resin from flowing past the edges of the wood, make a well by positioning painter's tape around the edges of each square. Tape around bottom edges, overlapping taped sides, to seal.

4. Follow the instructions, #082, to prepare the resin mixture.

5. Place the wood square on a flat, level surface. Immediately pour resin inside well to cover photo or handwriting sample to about ⅛ inch thickness. Allow to harden up to 72 hours to ensure a strong bond.

6. Peel off painter's tape. Sand sides with fine-grit sandpaper if desired.

085
lift lovely weights

Bring a little piece of the outdoors to a desktop with paperweights showcasing natural materials. Use a flexible silicon muffin pan for the mold, add epoxy resin, then drop collected items into the resin and allow it to harden before popping it out of the mold.

YOU WILL NEED

Basic casting resin supplies
  (see #082)

**Silicone muffin pan (Note: Use this
  pan only for resin, and not for food.)**

Tweezers

**Assorted items to encapsulate, such
  as dried flowers, leaves, shells,
  glitter, and small notes**

Note: Always work with resin in a well-ventilated area.

1. Follow the instructions, #082, to prepare the resin mixture. Coat muffin pan with mold release spray.

2. Pour resin mixture into the muffin compartment. Fill the compartment only to the level you wish to place the objects.

3. Immediately drop items to be encapsulated onto wet resin. Pour additional resin on top of items to cover. Add items until satisfied with the look. Be sure to cover items completely with resin.

4. Repeat for each paperweight. Allow to harden up to 72 hours to ensure a strong bond.

5. Remove paperweights from the muffin pan by pushing on the back of the compartment and popping out each paperweight.

086

form photo holders

Combine the beauty of a glittery insect-theme paperweight with a wire photo display.

YOU WILL NEED

5-inch-long wire

Basic resin casting supplies (see #082)

Silicone insect mold

Glitter

Drill

Crafts glue

Bend wire into a paper clip-style loop. Follow the paperweight instructions in #085 to fill a silicone insect mold coated with mold release spray with resin and glitter. When hard, drill a ½-inch-deep hole into the paperweight. Add glue to the straight end of the wire and insert wire into the hole.

087

spot your next pour

Impress guests by adding interest to a clear pitcher and glasses using adhesive circles and glass paint.

YOU WILL NEED
Glassware
Round labels
Foam pouncer
White glass paint

1. Encircle the outside of the glassware with a row of round labels.

2. Use a foam pouncer to apply white glass paint over the labels and up the sides of the glassware (A). Avoid the rims so paint will not be ingested when glassware is used. Carefully peel off the stickers while the paint is still wet (B), scratching off any paint that seeps underneath.

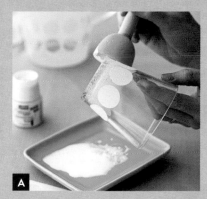

088
mold napkin rings

Personalize a table with handmade napkin rings.

YOU WILL NEED
Acrylic crafts paint
Basic casting resin supplies (see #082)
Rubber mold (designed for fondant)
Hot-glue gun and glue sticks
Napkin ring

Stir paint into a 1:1 mixture of resin and hardener (A). Coat mold with mold release spray. Pour resin into mold (B). Let dry for 24 hours. Remove the decoration from the mold before it has hardened. Carefully bend the pliable resin over the curve of the ring, hot-glue to the ring, then set aside for 48 hours to finish drying.

A

B

089

tack it up

To make these pretty pushpins, follow the technique and use the rubber molds from project #088. When resin is dry, affix the piece to the top of a thumbtack or magnet with hot glue.

090

play with paint

Tilting and swirling paint creates colorful vases that are unique every time you make one.

YOU WILL NEED

Enamel ceramic or glass paint
Glass vase

Pour a small amount of enamel into the bottom of the vase. Hold the vase in your hands and tip it in different directions so the paint rolls around inside, leaving some of the vase clear for interest. We don't recommend filling the vases with water after painting. It's best to use dried or fake flowers for decorating.

091
make your own milk glass

Save interesting bottles, glasses, and jars and swirl acrylic paint inside them to mimic the look of milk glass.

YOU WILL NEED

Glass bottle or jar

Rubbing alcohol and clean cloth

Acrylic paints (such as Martha Stewart Crafts Multi-Surface Acrylic Craft Paint) in desired colors

Glass bowl

Paper towel or paper plate

1. Wash glass with soap and water; dry. Dampen cloth with rubbing alcohol; wipe inside ot glass vessel with cloth. Pour a small amount of rubbing alcohol inside narrow vessels; swirl alcohol around inside of vessel, then pour out excess. Let air-dry.

2. In a glass bowl combine paint and water in a 2:1 ratio. Pour the mixture into the bottle or jar.

3. Swirl paint around inside bottle or jar until entire interior is coated.

4. Place glass vessel upside down on paper towel or paper plate; let dry.

5. Repeat Steps 2 to 4 several times until satisfied with coverage. We don't recommend filling the vases with water after painting. Use only dried or fake flowers for decorating.

092

seal everyday moments

Create a display for a treasured photo for gifting.

YOU WILL NEED

Photo

Decorative paper

Decoupage medium

Soap mold

Mold release spray

Basic casting resin supplies (see #082)

Toothpick

Mini easel

1. Cut out an image to desired size. Cut a paper circle the same shape and size as the cut photo from the decorative paper and adhere it to the back of the photo. Seal both sides with decoupage medium; let dry.

2. Spray a soap mold with mold release before adding a 1:1 mixture of resin and hardener, and the photo (A). Use a toothpick to embed the photo facedown in the resin (B). Let dry 24 hours before removing the frame from the mold.

3. To finish, cut decorative paper to fit the back of the frame and secure with spray adhesive. Display your project on a mini easel.

A

B

093

wrap a vase in a flash

Inspired by porch swings, this once-plain vase is a stunning accent.

YOU WILL NEED

Hot-glue gun and glue sticks

Thick rope

Hurricane vase

1. Use dots of hot glue to secure rope around the center of the vase.

2. Secure each end of the rope with a dot of glue.

094

catch some rays

Hung in a sunny window, this sea-glass-inspired mobile reflects light and color throughout a room.

YOU WILL NEED

Basic casting resin supplies (see #082)

Rubber ice cube trays

Food coloring

Screw eye

Fishing line

Metal ring

Coat ice cube trays with mold release spray. Pour a 1:1 mixture of resin and hardener into trays. Add one or two drops of food coloring to each mold and mix with a stir stick. Once dry, remove reflectors from the mold, then insert a screw eye into the top of each. Tie fishing line to the hooks and suspend the reflectors at varying heights from a metal ring.

095

preserve nature

Craft this pretty paperweight to secure stray documents on your desk or counter.

YOU WILL NEED
Basic casting resin supplies (see #82)
Plastic cup
Toothpick
Dried flowers

Pour resin into a plastic paint-mixing cup coated with mold release spray. Use a toothpick to "float" dried flowers in the resin at various levels for dimension. Let dry before popping the paperweight from its mold.

Painting & Stenciling

Simple paints and supplies can turn pillows, linens, containers, and more into gifts that rival the offerings from fancy boutiques.

096
stain a wooden tray

Pump up the style of an unfinished wooden tray with a herringbone stencil and colorful stain. Water-base stains such as Cabot Premium wood finish are available in a variety of vibrant colors that allow the wood grain to show through Although this product doesn't require wood conditioner and is a stain and sealer in one, apply an additional clear coat to the inside of the tray to protect the unstained wood. It is challenging to get crisp lines when stenciling with stain, so avoid intricate patterns.

YOU WILL NEED

Unfinished wood tray

180-grit sandpaper

Tack cloth

Crafts knife

Painter's tape

Water-base stain

Synthetic-bristle brush

Stencil

Repositionable spray adhesive

Natural sea sponge

Water-base clear finish

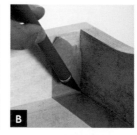  

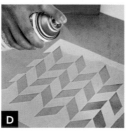  

1. Gather materials (A). Lightly sand the tray with 180-grit sandpaper, then remove dust with a tack cloth. Tape off the inside bottom of tray with painter's tape, trimming corners with a crafts knife (B).

2. Apply stain to tray sides with a synthetic-bristle brush (C).

3. Cut stencil to fit and coat the back with a thin layer of repositionable spray adhesive (D).

4. Remove painter's tape and position stencil on the tray. Press the edges down. Dip sponge in stain, blot excess on a paper towel, and stencil using a pouncing motion (E). Repeat with other colors as desired. Let dry for 2½ hours. Remove stencil. Allow stain to dry before repositioning stencil to avoid smearing.

5. Use a synthetic-bristle brush to seal the entire tray with a clear finish (F).

097

stamp on wall art

Design a custom stamp from materials you can find on your workbench.

YOU WILL NEED
Hot-glue gun and glue sticks
3 feet of ½-inch-wide cotton rope
Cardboard
Acrylic crafts paint
Card stock

Hot-glue rope onto a piece of cardboard in desired pattern. Lightly paint the rope with acrylic crafts paint and press it rope-side-down onto cardstock. For a two-tone look, repeat the process, twisting the block a quarter-turn, with a second color. Let dry, then frame.

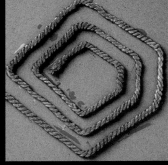

098
fish for compliments

This batik-inspired pillow sham will delight your favorite nature lover.

YOU WILL NEED

Fish pattern

Black marker

White pillow sham

Elmer's washable glue

Fabric paint

Paintbrush

Rag

1. Make a fish pattern from clip art or a freehand sketch. Outline with a bold black marker.

2. Place the pattern inside the pillow sham, and trace it on the fabric with glue (A) to make a mask. After the glue dries (it will turn white), brush on the color using a slightly watered-down fabric paint (B). For the blue splatter look on the pillowcase, right, experiment with splattering or spraying thinned fabric paint.

3. When the paint dries completely, soak the sham in water and gently rub away the glue. To set your design, follow the fabric paint directions, but not before removing the glue.

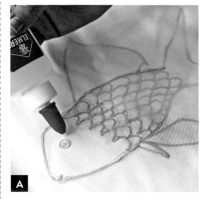

A

B

099
flag the perfect gift

A plain purchased banner is a canvas for customizing, and the addition of paint on the pennant tips gives it a modern edge.

YOU WILL NEED

2 purchased burlap pennant banners

1 purchased vellum pennant banner (our pennants have gold-tone borders)

Crafts glue

Hole punch

Shallow, wide container

Fingernail polish: pink, black, white, seafoam green

Bamboo skewer

1 yard natural-and-gold twine

1. Remove the hanging strings from the burlap and the vellum pennants.

2. Run a line of crafts glue along the back edges of a vellum pennant, and adhere a vellum pennant to half of the burlap pennants, aligning top edges. Let dry.

3. Punch a hole at the top corners of each pennant.

4. Fill a container with water 5 to 6 inches deep. Drizzle each fingernail polish color onto the surface of the water. Use a bamboo skewer to gently swirl the colors on the water.

5. Dip the burlap-only pennant tips into the water and quickly lift them out. Repeat as desired, swirling the colors and adding more polish to the water as needed between pennants. Let the pennants dry. Thread the pennants onto the twine, alternating a burlap-only pennant with a vellum-and-burlap pennant.

100
pretty up napkins with block-print

Look around your house to find interesting print-worthy objects. Buttons, with their tiny details, make a big impact on cloth napkins, but you could also use paper clips, safety pins, or other small items.

YOU WILL NEED

Hot-glue gun and glue sticks

Small wood block

Fabric paint

Button

Scrap fabric

Fabric napkins

Hot-glue a button onto a wooden block, then dab an even layer of fabric paint onto the button. Practice pressing the design onto a scrap of fabric to make sure you're happy with the results before stamping onto the napkin. If your button has a shank, carve a small space for it out of the wood block or stick the button into an eraser and stamp away. Heat-set the designs according to the paint manufacturer's instructions.

Tip: Choose fabric with a smooth texture for crisper prints.

101

stamp a rosy runner

Go big or go home with large-scale designs cut from crafts foam and stamped on a fabric table runner.

YOU WILL NEED
Scrap paper
Sticky-backed crafts foam
Scissors
Large wood block
Screen-printing ink for fabric
Fabric table runner

1. Draw a design on paper and use it as a template to trace onto sticky-backed crafts foam (A). Cut your design, peel off the backing, and adhere the pieces to a large wood block or the bottom of a cake pan (B).

2. Roll an even layer of screen-printing ink for fabric over the design, then press it onto the fabric, applying even pressure. Hold the fabric down as you lift the stamp to prevent sticking and smudging. Rinse off the foam and let dry between impressions to ensure crisp lines.

A

B

102
embellish a tea towel

A cotton flour sack towel gets a strawberry-sweet makeover with a block-printed design.

YOU WILL NEED

Printmaking carving block

Linoleum cutter

Screen-printing ink for fabric

Brayer

Tea towel

Iron

Freehand a design onto the carving block. To get a textured look, partially carve away sections of the space around the main design (A). Roll an even layer of screen-printing ink for fabric over the design with a brayer (B). Flip the block and press it evenly onto the fabric to transfer the image. After ink dries, heat-set by ironing the reverse side of the towel at the highest setting for the fabric type or placing the towel in a dryer for a few minutes.

A

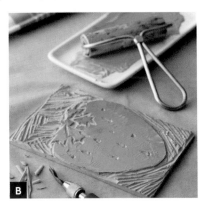

B

103
carve a pillow print

A repeating floral design on a plain cotton pillow cover looks like designer fabric.

YOU WILL NEED
Pillow form
Fabric pillow cover
Ink-jet-printed design
Printmaking carving block
Iron
Linoleum cutter
Screen-printing ink for fabric
Brayer

1. Remove the pillow form from the cover. Slip a piece of cardboard inside to prevent the ink from bleeding through. Place an ink-jet-printed design facedown onto the printmaking carving block, and use an iron on warm setting to transfer the design.

2. Remove the negative space using a linoleum cutter; push and scoop out the linoleum, pointing the sharp end of the cutter away from you.

3. Roll an even layer of screen-printing ink for fabric over the design with a brayer, then press the block evenly onto the pillow cover, starting at the center. Repeat, working toward the edges and reapplying ink after each print. For cleaner results, take time to wipe away excess paint from the block between each impression.

4. After ink dries, heat-set by ironing on the reverse side of the pillow cover at the highest setting for the fabric type or by placing the pillow cover in the dryer for a few minutes.

4 Ways to Gift with Chalkboard Paint

104
give the gift of organization

Create a personalized set of office-supply storage with three simple ingredients: glass jars, spray chalkboard paint, and a chalk pen. Spray the jars with a few coats of chalkboard paint. Label the jar with a chalk pen. For a consistent look, use white adhesive letters instead of the chalk pen.

105
customize a chalk banner

Create a banner with a personalized message. Layer a chalkboard fabric hexagon atop a 5-inch diameter print cardstock circle. Stitch together ¼-inch inside hexagon edges, pivoting at corners and backstitching at last corner, to make a circle unit. Use 2 inches of Velcro Sew On Snag Free Tape on the back to attach to a ribbon. Customize the banner to spell your desired message with chalk.

106
make a traveling chalkboard

Give the gift of quiet entertainment to the kiddos on your list with this custom—and travel-friendly—chalkboard. Apply three or four coats of chalkboard paint to a thin wood shape from the crafts store. Use a scrap of fabric to secure a muslin pouch holding chalk and an eraser.

107
serve up some photos

Give a tray a fun interactive element with chalkboard paint on the flat, interior surface. Once painted, wrap picture-hanging wire through the handles and across the tray front. Twist the wire ends together on the back of the tray. Mini clothespins make perfect picture hangers.

dilute dye for a dreamy look

The shams look like they were treated to a resist effect, but diluted dye applied over a stencil produces the soft, muted, dreamy look.

YOU WILL NEED
Cardboard
White cotton pillow sham
Fabric dye
Spray adhesive
Stencil
Paintbrush

1. Insert a piece of cardboard between the layers of a white cotton pillow sham to prevent dye from bleeding through to the back.

2. Use spray adhesive to adhere the stencil to fabric, and spritz fabric with water before brushing on color.

109
mark your place

Painter's tape is the key to the crisp dividing line between painted and natural finishes on these plywood place mats.

YOU WILL NEED

¼-inch-thick birch plywood

¾-inch-wide birch veneer

Iron

Crafts knife

Sandpaper

Painter's tape

Acrylic crafts paint

Paintbrush or roller

Polyurethane or other clear coat

Self-adhesive felt pads (made to protect wood floors from furniture scuffs)

1. Cut ¼-inch-thick birch plywood into six 15-inch squares. (If you don't have a table saw or circular saw, ask a hardware store to cut the wood for you.)

2. Following manufacturer's instructions, use an iron to apply birch veneer to edges of each plywood square (A). For the least waste, clamp together three squares at a time and apply a single ¾-inch-wide strip of veneer.

3. Using a crafts knife, cut apart plywood squares (B). Use sandpaper to sand cut edges for a smooth, seamless finish.

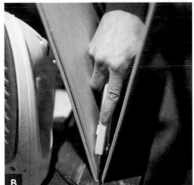

4. Mask off one diagonal half of each plywood square with a strip of painter's tape. Using a paintbrush or roller, cover one half of the square with two coats of paint (C). Peel off the tape while the second coat is wet to ensure a clean line. Once the paint is completely dry, apply three coats of polyurethane. Add a felt pad to the underside of each place mat at each corner to slightly float it off the table and protect your surface.

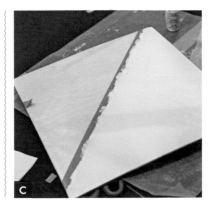

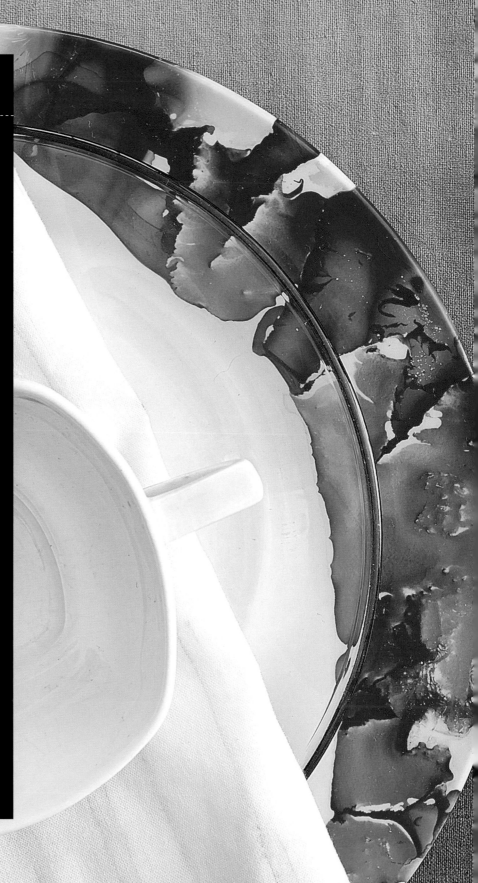

perk up plates

Imperfect splashes of color on inexpensive dishes bring a lively touch to a table.

YOU WILL NEED
Nail polish
Plastic container
Plates

Drizzle nail polish into water in a plastic container (A). (For the best results, drizzle the polish in a zigzag motion.) Immediately dip a portion of a plate, saucer, or bowl through the polish in the water, and pull it out (B). Work quickly before the polish hardens in the water.

Note: Color only the areas where food will not touch or top with clear glass plates. Hand-wash only.

A

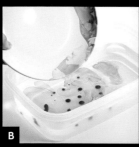

B

111
print nifty napkins

As an alternative to stamping, use a version of screen printing to customize napkins.

YOU WILL NEED (for six napkins)

1⅞ yards solid-white cotton fabric

Self-adhesive stencil film

Crafts knife

Temporary spray adhesive or masking tape

Kraft paper

Fabric paint (or acrylic crafts paint with textile medium added)

Stencil brush

Iron

Finished Napkin: 19 inches square

1. Wash and dry solid-white fabric; press flat. Cut into six 21-inch squares.

2. Enlarge and trace pattern on Pattern Page C onto self-adhesive stencil film, tracing dashed lines and gray shapes. Using a crafts knife, cut out only gray shapes. (Dashed lines are for aligning with previously stamped plus signs.)

3. Cover work surface with kraft paper. Use temporary spray adhesive or masking tape to secure one fabric square to work surface.

4. Position stencil in upper left-hand corner of fabric square and secure. Dip stencil brush in fabric paint; blot off most of it. Tap paint within the stencil until area is covered. Apply the paint in several thin coats to work it into the fibers. Carefully lift the stencil, making sure not to smudge the paint on the fabric. When paint is dry, position stencil to right of first set of plus signs, aligning dashed lines with first plus signs. Repeat to stamp remaining plus signs, working across then down the fabric square. Heat-set with an iron if required.

5. On each edge of stamped fabric, turn under ½ inch twice and press. Stitch close to first folded edge to complete napkin.

sprinkle on sparkle

Give letter stickers a new look and purpose by using them as masks for kitchen canister lettering to keep essentials looking their best.

YOU WILL NEED
White ceramic canisters
1½-inch-tall letter stickers
**Fine-tip oil-base markers: gold
   and brown**

1. Adhere letter stickers to the sides of white ceramic canisters to spell the word coffee, flour, and sugar.

2. Use gold and brown fine-tip oil-base markers to add closely spaced dots around letter stickers; let dry.

3. Carefully remove letter stickers.

raise a glass

Customize a set of cocktail glasses for giving with just a few materials and a few minutes.

YOU WILL NEED
Painter's tape
Credit card
Cocktail glasses
Acrylic crafts paint

1. Use painter's tape (rubbed with a credit card for a secure seal) to mark a line on two inexpensive glasses.

2. Apply two or three coats of acrylic crafts paint suitable for glass, and gift as a set. (Follow paint instructions for curing time before washing.)

Paper, Wood & Metal

Share intriguing textures and charming details in this collection of crafts made with materials inspired by nature and traditional handiwork.

114

craft a crepe paper wreath

Let the spirit of spring thrive indoors year-round with these paper peonies.

YOU WILL NEED
Scissors
Fine crepe paper
20-gauge wire
Green paper twist
Hot-glue gun and glue sticks
Green florist tape
Tissue paper
Foam wreath form

1. Cut a 2×10-inch strip of crepe paper along the grain; fold in half. Fringe the folded side of about ½ inch. Cut a 6-inch piece of wire for the stem. Dab some hot glue onto the top of the stem, secure on one narrow end of the yellow paper, and roll, fanning the paper outward. Dab opposite end with glue and secure to stem with tape.

2. Using the patterns on Page Pattern C, cut out six small and six large petals from crepe paper. Pinch the bottom of the small petals together, then tape to the wire stem, filling in empty spaces. Continue layering large petals to finish each flower.

3. To make a peony bud, bunch a piece of tissue paper. Cut a 3×3-inch piece of fine crepe paper. Cover the tissue paper ball with the crepe paper and attach to a 6-inch length of 20-gauge wire with green florist tape. Cut a 4-inch piece of green paper twist and unravel halfway. Cut a scallop at the top. Wrap around the bud and hot-glue to the stem. Arrange the pieces on a foam wreath form wrapped in green paper twist. Secure with hot glue. This 12-inch wreath is made with 17 flowers and five buds.

crepe paper tips

If you make a lot of paper flowers, here are the materials that are good to have on hand:

Doublet crepe paper: Two sheets of fine crepe paper are laminated together to form this smooth paper.

Fine crepe paper: This nearly sheer paper is perfect for delicate parts of a flower.

Florist crepe paper: Available in 160- and 180-gram weights, this is slightly thicker than fine crepe paper and is ideal for petal making.

Flower centers: Found in the florist aisle of a crafts store, these wire embellishments add a realistic appearance to the paper flowers.

20-gauge florist wire: This thin and delicate wire is used as the stem of flowers or to secure a flower when more support is needed.

26-gauge florist wire: Slightly thinner and more flexible, this wire is useful for holding the center of flowers together—or for a stem that needs flexibility. It is sold with or without cloth covering.

Green and white florist tape: To make the wire look like a stem and to secure the base of the flowers, each is wrapped in either white or green florist tape.

115
put spring in someone's step

Dress up flats with this delicate floral clip.

YOU WILL NEED

Scissors

Fine crepe paper

Flower centers

26-gauge wire

Gold tulle

160-gram crepe paper

White florist tape

Hot-glue gun and glue sticks

Shoe clip

Cut a 2×12-inch strip of fine crepe paper. Fringe each side. Pinch strip together, add a few flower centers, and wrap center with an 8-inch length of 26-gauge wire to secure. Fluff crepe paper. Cut a 2-inch square of gold tulle, pinch center, and use wire to secure. Cut a 2½-inch square of yellow 160-gram crepe paper and cut out leaf shapes. Pinch the center of the base and use wire to secure. Gather the three bunches in a stack (leaves on bottom, gold in middle, fringe on top) and secure wires together with white florist tape. Glue to a shoe clip.

116
brooch the subject

Adorn a blouse, sweater, or dress with this pretty paper pin.

YOU WILL NEED
Scissors
Fine crepe paper
26-gauge wire
Green paper twist
Pin back or brooch clip

1. Cut a 13×4-inch piece of fine crepe paper. Fold in half widthwise, so that it is 6.5×4-inches, then in half widthwise again, so that it is 3.25×4-inches. Cut out six petals on each of the non-folded, 4-inch sides as shown. Open, gather together, pinch center, and wrap with an 8-inch length of 26-gage wire to secure.

2. For the center of the flower, cut a 9×1-inch strip of fine crepe paper. Fringe each side. Pinch center, gather together, and wrap with an 8-inch length of 26-gauge wire. For the leaf, cut a 6-inch length of green paper twist. Leaving the ends twisted, flatten the center of the piece to create a leaf shape.

3. Layer the center of the flower over the center of the petals and use the wires to poke a hole through the center of the leaf; pull through. Fluff to form the flower. Twist wire around a pin back or brooch clip to secure, trimming wire to finish.

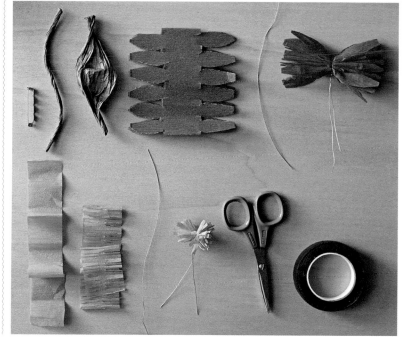

BLACKBERRIES = PURPLE

PINK FLOWERS
& LEAVES = PINK

TURMERIC = YELLOW

know dyeing basics

Before you begin, acquire steel and enamelware pots and pans (aluminum, copper, and iron can affect the dye color) as well as glass bowls, a large metal spoon, mesh strainers, and measuring cups and spoons. Wear an apron and waterproof gloves; cover counters and flooring with drop cloths.

1. Prepare fibers: Wrap yarn, cord, twine, lace, or other trims into loose skeins. Prewash and rinse by hand to remove any residue. To wash, cover the material with water; for each gallon of water, add 1 teaspoon of pH-neutral soap and 1 tablespoon washing soda. Rinse.

2. Enhance brightness, evenness, and light- and wash-fastness: In a large pot, dissolve ¼ cup of alum plus 1 tablespoon cream of tartar in 4 gallons of water per 1 pound of fibers. Add fibers. Heat to simmer for 1 hour, let cool, and rinse.

3. Make dye: Simmer 1 cup chopped plant material in 2 cups water for 20 to 45 minutes. The longer the material is simmered, the more the dye color intensifies. Strain, then allow to cool for cool-dye method or continue simmering for hot-dye method. Gradually move fibers from one bath to another—wash, mordant (a fixative that "sets" the color), dye, and rinse—cool to warm and warm to cool.

117

dip in natural dye

Subtle colors and wooden beads pair up to make a modern statement in this pretty necklace.

YOU WILL NEED

Wood beads

Alum (aluminum sulfate from a garden center)

1- or 2-quart pan

Enamelware or glass bowls

Turmeric powder

Blackberries

Pink flowers and leaves

Fine-mesh strainer

String

1. Soak the beads overnight in a solution of 1 teaspoon alum dissolved in 2 cups water; let them dry before dyeing. For yellow dye, dissolve 3 tablespoons turmeric powder in 1 cup water. For purple dye, stir 1 cup water into ½ cup crushed blackberries. For pink dye, simmer 1 cup chopped pink flowers and leaves (such as rose, begonia, cosmos, coleus) in 2 cups water for 30 to 45 minutes; strain the solution and let it cool. Strong dye baths yield the best results when cool-bath dyeing.

2. Soak the wood beads in each dye bath overnight. (Dyeing the beads for two days will intensify their color.) Stir the dye bath occasionally to ensure even dyeing. Place dyed beads in a strainer, rinse under cool running water, and set aside to dry. Use the beads to string a colorful necklace.

Note: Cool-bath dyeing also works well for wool and silk. Some plants produce good results with a cool-dye.

119
paint pretty rocks

Even better than the pet rocks of childhood, this collection of smooth river rocks features upscale organic motifs drawn on the surfaces.

YOU WILL NEED

Assorted smooth river rocks: dark gray and light gray

Extra-fine-tip oil-base markers: white and gold

Painter's tape

Acrylic paint

1. Wash river rocks with water; let dry.

2. Using a white oil-base marker and referring to the photograph for inspiration, draw simple organic shapes—such as leaves, geometric patterns, or words—on rocks. Let dry.

3. For stripes, use painter's tape to mask off a portion of chosen rocks. Paint unmasked area with acrylic paint; let dry. If needed, apply a second coat of paint; let dry. Remove painter's tape and use gold or white oil-base markers to color unpainted areas.

marker tip
The Sharpie white, extra-fine marking pen is the perfect tool for doodling detailed designs on rocks; sharpie.com

120

tile art work

This collection of children's art in a poster frame is the perfect gift for grandparents.

YOU WILL NEED
Art work
Computer
Frame

Scan art pieces, then import them into an image-editing program. Crop and shrink art to desired size, then place the images in a gridded layout. Take the file to a print shop and request a poster-size print to frame and hang.

121
frame a rainbow

Capture a moment in time with a framed silhouette of your child as a gift for a parent or grandparent.

YOU WILL NEED

Camera

Plain printer paper

Black marker

Watercolor art by your child (preferably done on thick watercolor paper)

Crafts knife or fine-tip scissors

1. Snap a photo of your child's profile (it works best against a plain background, like a wall or sheet). Using printer paper, print the photo in a size smaller than the artwork you wish to feature.

2. Roughly trace around your child's head on the photo with a black marker. Lay a sheet of printer paper over the photo, and trace a clean outline using a black marker. Place this paper over watercolor art. Holding the papers up to a brightly lit window, trace the silhouette using a pencil.

3. Cut the shape from the watercolor art using a crafts knife or fine-tip scissors; start cutting at the center and pay close attention to details such as hair, lips, and eyelashes. Flip the sheet over (or erase all pencil marks) and label the bottom with your child's name and age. Mount it to the painting with spray adhesive or double-stick tape, then frame.

122

show off silhouettes

Make use of patterned paper and color for a contemporary twist on the classic silhouette.

YOU WILL NEED

Tracing paper

Spray adhesive

Decorative paper

Scissors

Frame

1. Trace the outline of a family photo on tracing paper. Lightly spray the back of the tracing with adhesive and smooth it onto the back of decorative paper. Cut out the shape using sharp scissors.

2. Turn over the silhouette and adhere it to a background paper cut to fit your frame.

4 Ways to Gift Tree Slices

123
stencil a set

Give a nature lover a little something to bring the woods indoors. Tree branch segments are available as pre-cut slices at crafts stores, so there's no need for a saw. Simply stencil fox, mushroom, and branch motifs (or other nature-themed motifs) onto tree branch segments with acrylic paint; let dry. Add picture hanging brackets to the back if necessary.

124
wood-burn a wall sign

Inspire a friend or family member with a personalized message on a wood-burned plaque. (Wood burning, also known as pyrography, is a process in which a light, gliding touch is used to move a hot penlike tool over wood to create custom designs. See #130 for tools and instructions on wood burning.) In this project, colorful painted flowers and leaves complement burned branch and leaf outlines around the perimeter. Add picture-hanging brackets to the back if necessary.

125
gift a gem
Combine a contemporary image with a rustic slice of wood for a fresh piece of giftable art. Map out a gem shape on a wood slice with a pencil, then guide the straight-edge tip of a wood-burning pen along the lines (see #130 for tools and instructions on wood burning). Tightly secure painter's tape around the two right-edge triangle shapes of the gem. Brush on metallic acrylic paint, remove the tape, and let dry. Add picture hanging brackets to the back if necessary.

126
coast with the grain
These thick watercolor coasters provide durable protection against damaging water rings. To make them, add a few drops of food coloring to ½ cup of water. Stir until mixed. Make several colors, if desired. Dip paper towels into water. Drip color onto wood slices. Add more colors, if desired. Let dry. Apply clear protective finish with a paintbrush. Let dry. Add self-adhesive felt pads to undersides.

127
get a handle on it

Serve breakfast in bed (or afternoon tea) on a custom tray.

YOU WILL NEED

12×16×1½-inch basswood canvas with sides

Clamps

Scrap wood blocks

Drill and corresponding bit

Wood screws

Crafts paint

Peel-and-stick wallpaper

Cabinet drawer pulls

1. Mark the positions of the drawer pull holes on one narrow side of the basswood canvas.

2. Clamp scrap wood blocks along the inside edge for splinter-free exiting of the drill bit (see photo). Drill holes.

3. Prime and paint the canvas. Cut wallpaper to line the tray bottom. Smooth in place.

4. Attach drawer handles with a screwdriver to finish.

128
let there be light

Light up someone's life with a
custom-made night-light.

YOU WILL NEED
Small plate
Awl
Scrap wood
**12×12×1¾-inch basswood canvas
  with sides**
Drill and corresponding bit
White LED string lights

1. Trace a small plate onto paper to
help fashion a starburst. Create your
own pattern or use the pattern on
Pattern Page B, making sure the
number of dots you create doesn't
exceed the number of lights on the
string. Protect your work surface
with a scrap of thick wood or a
cutting board.

2. To transfer a design to the face of
the canvas, use an awl to gently
press pilot holes at the dots (A).
Practice on scrap wood first if
desired. Drill pilot holes at the awl
marks using a bit slightly smaller than
the individual lightbulb (B).

3. Using a drill bit the size of the bulbs,
enlarge the holes. Poke lights through
the design from the back (C). Plug in.

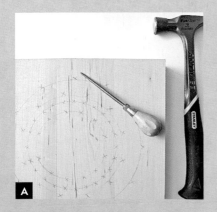

A

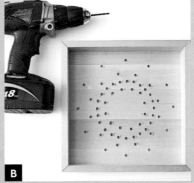

B

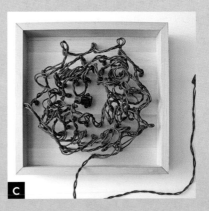

C

129
mat a map

An inexpensive map becomes eye-catching art when you layer hand-cut watercolor paper on top.

YOU WILL NEED

Map
24×36-inch white foam-core board
Rubber cement
Crafts knife
Metal ruler
Cutting mat
24×36-inch watercolor paper
Graphite paper
Letter stencils

1. Assemble supplies (A). Dry-mount the map to the foam-core board by applying a layer of rubber cement to both surfaces, letting it dry, and pressing the surfaces together. Trim any overhanging map with a crafts knife and ruler on a cutting mat.

2. Trace the letters backwards onto the watercolor paper using the graphite paper (B). Cut out, using the ruler for straight edges (C). Discard inside pieces.

3. Using the dry-mount technique, glue the watercolor paper to the map board, lining up the edges. Trim any overhanging paper with a ruler and crafts knife.

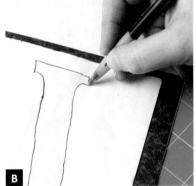

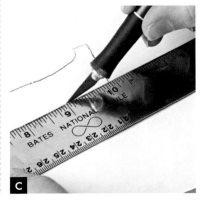

130
wood-burn a treasure trove

Transform a blank box into a covetable accessory with a wood-burning technique.

YOU WILL NEED

4-inch flower stencil (such as Plaid Folk Art Home Decor Stencil: Camelia)

Stencil plastic and crafts knife (optional)

Small hexagon wooden box (featured box is 3×5½×5½ inches)

Wood-burning tool (such as Walnut Hollow Creative Woodburner)

Wood-burning tip: narrow cone point (such as Walnut Hollow tips)

Wood stain (such as Minwax Wood Finish in Golden Pecan)

Polyurethane sealer spray: clear satin

1. Position the stencil on the center of the box lid. Lightly trace the stencil openings using a pencil.

2. Trace lines using a wood-burning tool fitted with a narrow cone point. Erase any visible pencil marks.

3. Dip a cloth in a small amount of wood stain and rub stain onto all outer surfaces of the box; let dry.

4. Spray the box with polyurethane sealer spray; let dry.

HOW TO USE A WOOD-BURNING TOOL

1. Trace, transfer, or draw a motif onto the surface you wish to burn, such as wood or leather.

2. Place the desired tip on the wood-burning pen, then turn on the pen. Trace the motif with the hot pen. The longer you hold the tip of the pen in place, the darker and deeper the burn.

131

serve up sweetness

Give the gift of custom made cooking tools with a simple, yet impressive, technique.

YOU WILL NEED

Wooden spoon

Wood-burning tool (such as Walnut Hollow Creative Woodburner)

Wood-burning tip: narrow cone point (such as Walnut Hollow tips)

1. Draw a heart with a pencil on a wooden spoon. Use the pencil-thin pointed tip of a wood-burning tool (see #130) to dot around the shape. Cluster the dots close to the outline, spreading them apart as you work outward.

2. Write a message with pencil on the handle and trace using the same tip; erase pencil lines. For the geometric take, use a metal ruler to draw straight lines on the spoon. With consistent, light pressure, guide the straight-edge tip across the lines.

3. To make the sugar canister, follow the instructions in Step 2.

132
silhouette some coasters

Make a set of coordinating coasters by burning shapely silhouettes of people and animals onto the centers of square wooden plaques.

YOU WILL NEED

4-inch-square wooden plaques

Wood-burning pen (such as Walnut Hollow Creative Woodburner)

Wood-burning tips: narrow cone and flow points (such as Walnut Hollow tips)

Polyurethane spray sealer: glossy

Acrylic paint: gray

Small paintbrush

⅜-inch-diameter adhesive-back felt circles (four for each coaster)

1. Find free silhouette clip art online, and print it onto heavy white paper; cut it out. Lightly trace each shape onto the center of a wooden plaque using a pencil.

2. Trace the pencil lines using a wood-burning pen fitted with a narrow cone point (see #130).

3. Use a flow point tip to fill in the outlines and burn entire silhouettes.

4. Spray glossy polyurethane sealer on each coaster; let dry. Apply a second coat; let dry.

5. Paint the beveled edges of each coaster gray; let dry.

6. Spray a final coat of glossy polyurethane sealer on each coaster; let dry.

7. Adhere four felt circles to the bottom of each coaster.

133

craft wooden jewelry wonders

Transform wooden beads into creative accessories with freehand wood-burning embellishments.

YOU WILL NEED

Wood-burning pen (such as Walnut Hollow Creative Woodburner)

Wood-burning tips: flow point and cone point (such as Walnut Hollow tips)

8 to 10 colored wooden beads ranging in size from ¾ inch to 1 inch

2-inch-round wooden disk

Transfer paper

Drill with ⅛-inch bit

2 coordinating filler beads with small holes

Suede necklace cord

Jewelry pliers

2 crimp ends with loops

2 split rings

Lobster clasp

Rat tail cording or jewelry chain

1. Place desired wood-burning tip on the wood-burning pen. Freehand-draw lines, squiggles, dots, and letters onto the beads.

2. Place transfer paper on top of the wooden disc. Place the pendant pattern on Pattern Page B on the transfer paper. Using the blunt end of a ballpoint pen, trace the pattern to transfer it onto the wooden disk.

3. Burn the design lines on the wooden disk using a wood-burning pen fitted with a cone point.

4. Drill two holes spaced approximately ⅜ inch apart at the top of the disk.

5. Cut a necklace cord to desired length. Thread the cord ends from front to back through the holes in the disk. Adjust the cord so ends are even and the cord lays flat between the holes on the front of the disk.

6. Tie an overhand knot in the cord along each side of the wooden disk. Thread a filler bead onto each cord end; the knots should prevent the beads from touching the disk.

7. Thread wood-burned beads onto cord ends. Arrange the beads to create a balanced design on each side of the disk.

8. Using jewelry pliers, attach crimp ends to each cord end. Attach a split ring to each loop on the crimp ends.

9. Attach a lobster clasp to one split ring. Cut a 6-inch length of rat tail cording; attach to remaining split ring.

10. Fit necklace around your neck; adjust the chain length as needed by cutting off excess. Leave about 3 inches of cording for adjustments.

134

build a bouquet

Raid your jewelry box or pick up thrift-shop finds to make a stunning floral arrangement that will never wilt. Thread a piece of wire through the back of each brooch, earring, or pendant, and wrap the wires with florist tape to create stems. Insert the wire stems in a piece of florist foam, and place the arrangement in a vase.

135
take note

Your friend can keep track of memories, to-do lists, or things she is grateful for with a sweet handmade notebook.

YOU WILL NEED
Cardstock
Crafts knife
Self-healing mat
Clear gridded ruler
Fabric
Pinking shears
Decoupage medium
Foam brush
Yarn
Sharp darning or embroidery needle
Small nameplate

1. Cut sheets of cardstock to 5½×8½ inches using a crafts knife, clear gridded ruler, and self-healing mat. Cut an additional piece of 5¾×8¾-inch cardstock for the cover; set aside. Fold each of the smaller pieces in half, pressing a sharp crease.

2. Cut a piece of fabric to 6¾×18½ inches using pinking shears. Use decoupage medium to secure the fabric to the cover on all sides, folding the fabric at the corners as if wrapping a present. Apply more decoupage medium over the tops of the corners for extra security. Let dry. Crease cover. Stack the pages on the cover, positioning the interior papers evenly. Thread yarn through two holes in the spine with a sharp darning or embroidery needle. Tie to secure the pages to the cover. Add a name plate and insert a label.

Plants, Bouquets & Mini Gardens

Add blooming freshness to a loved one's life with the gift of green. Think pretty plants, embellished containers, whimsical terrariums, and more.

136

form a
lovely letter

Cluster blooms in tiny jars within a favorite letter form to create a charming party centerpiece perfect for a wedding shower or birthday.

YOU WILL NEED

Small vases or votive holders

Letter form (available at crafts stores)

Flowers of your choice

Arrange the vases around the letter form. Fill with flowers cut down to fit. One main color accented with a few contrasting bursts makes a big impact.

137

hang a macramé planter

A simple tying technique transforms cording into a statement piece.

YOU WILL NEED

10 yards of cording, twine, or paracord

1¼-inch metal ring or key ring

6-inch-tall ceramic planter

1. Cut four 90-inch-long cording strands and lay together in a group. Thread all through the metal ring. Tie the centers to the ring (Diagram 1).

2. Split the strands into four sections, two strands each. Tie each section with an overhand knot about 8 inches below top knot (Diagram 2).

3. Split the tails below each knot and join tails from adjacent knots with an overhand knot approximately 3 to 4 inches below the knots from Step 2 (Diagram 3).

4. Group all tails together and knot them with a large overhand knot that will hold the planter in place (Diagram 4).

5. Insert planter into hanger. Trim tails to desired length.

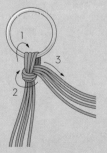

DIAGRAM 1

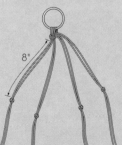

DIAGRAM 2

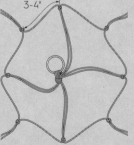

3-4"

DIAGRAM 3

DIAGRAM 4

138

sweater-wrap flowers

YOU WILL NEED

Sweater (felted or unfelted)

Ribbing from coordinating sweater or cording

1. Cut two 11-inch squares from a sweater, matching any patterns you choose. If you are not using a felted sweater, when cutting the squares, be sure the top edge of the finished bag is at the ribbing (bottom hem) of the sweater so this edge does not need to be finished.

2. With right sides together, use ½-inch seam to sew side and bottom edges, rounding the bottom corners as you sew.

3. To make a tie from cording, weave 35 inches of cording through the knit of the sweater about 2½ inches from top of bag; begin and end in center of one side of bag. To make a tie from ribbing, cut a 1×20-inch or larger piece of ribbing; hand-sew center of ribbing in place in back center of bag about 2½ inches from top of bag.

139
wind up a planter

Wrap a plain terra-cotta or plastic flowerpot with rope and accent it with a swath of paint to create a rustic vessel for a potted plant.

YOU WILL NEED
Hot-glue gun and glue sticks
Flowerpot
Rope or sisal twine
Latex paint
1-inch paintbrush

1. Place a 2-inch-long bead of glue along the bottom edge of the container. Quickly press the rope into the glue, holding it in place for a few seconds until the glue hardens slightly. Work in 2-inch segments to ensure the rope bonds to the pot before the glue dries.

2. Continue the process as you move up the container. Place each layer of twine as close to the previous as possible, gluing the rope to both the pot and the previous layer.

3. Create a band of color by painting several rows of rope with latex paint. Let dry. Add a second coat of paint if necessary to achieve the desired look.

4 Ways to Gift a Potted Plant

140
go nuts for monochrome
Add texture to plain containers with hex nuts. Lay a planter on its side and arrange hex nuts in a pattern, working in sections. Experiment with different sizes and shapes of nuts or washers. Spread a thin layer of glue over a small area and place hardware. Make sure to choose an adhesive that works outdoors and for the type of materials you're bonding. (On this project, Liquid Nails was used to bond metal to ceramic.) Once dry, spray-paint the entire planter for a chic monochromatic look.

141
roll with it
Casters turn a galvanized tub into a garden on wheels. Tape off sections of the tub to paint. Prime and paint with indoor/outdoor spray paint. Let dry, and remove tape. Arrange four swivel casters, evenly spaced, around the perimeter of the tub bottom. Mark the holes, set aside casters, and drill. Attach casters with bolts and nuts. Drill additional holes for drainage.

142
paint a pretty pot
Use painter's tape to create an asymmetrical design on a pot. Secure edges by rubbing with a credit card. Paint one side with multi-surface crafts paint; let dry. Remove tape and add the second paint color. Add additional coats as needed.

143
address a plain pot
Customize an ordinary terra-cotta pot with stencils. Use a house number, monogram, or a favorite symbol. Spray the inside of the pot with water sealant to keep the exterior paint from peeling. Let dry. Prime and spray-paint the pot exterior and a few inches inside the rim; let dry. Apply spray adhesive to the back of stencils, and position on pot. Mask area around stencil, and spray-paint numbers using light coats, letting dry between coats, until desired coverage is achieved. Remove stencils.

144

bring a wreath to life

Humble houseplants form a wondrous wreath that will live as happily indoors near a sunny window as it will outdoors in a shaded spot in spring. Include a note with the wreath to take it to a sink once a week for a thorough watering.

YOU WILL NEED

18 polka-dot plants (*Hypoestes phyllostachya*)

Jute liner

16-inch-diameter living wreath

Potting mix

Preserved moss

1. Round up materials, including 4-inch (or smaller) pots of polka-dot plant varieties in white and pink hues. Water the plants the day before assembling the wreath. Press the liner into the wire wreath form.

2. Unpot the plants, loosening and removing extra soil and tightly coiled roots (A). Begin fitting plants around the wreath perimeter, tucking the root balls through openings cut in the liner (B). Alternate plant colors pleasingly. Plant one-third of the wreath perimeter (C).

3. Plant one-third of the wreath front. Leave growing room between the root balls, depending on the number of plants and their size (D). Cover the root balls with potting mix.

4. Plant the second and third portions of the wreath in the same manner. Secure the potting mix by adding a front liner. Cut a 2-inch slit in the jute liner (E), then gently guide a plant through. Repeat for each plant. Fill any bare spots with bits of preserved moss.

5. Slide the top of the wreath form in place, guiding plants through the openings, and hook it on the base (F).

145

box up a whimsical forest

Arranging natural treasures in a shadow box creates a miniature whimsical world.

YOU WILL NEED

Wood screws

18×22-inch picture frame

2×2s cut to fit frame

¼-inch plywood

Sheet moss

Construction adhesive

Driftwood, ferns, lichen, mosses, and air plants

1. Use wood screws to attach a frame of 2×2s and a back of plywood to the purchased picture frame (see photo).

2. Secure sheet moss in place with construction adhesive. Add driftwood, preserved ferns, lichen, and colorful mosses. To finish, layer on air plants to where they can be removed easily for weekly watering.

146

put on the glitz

Dress up common houseplants in minutes with simple accessories that quick-change for any occasion.

YOU WILL NEED
Die-cut place mat
Florist wire

Gather the die-cut place mat around the pot and secure the folds with bits of wire as desired.

147
create a tiny world

Terrariums are endlessly fascinating both to children and adults. Make a living gift for someone special that reflects their interests and passions. They can be closed with a lid or left open and you can place them on a shelf or table or hang on a rope. Keep your terrarium moist with a spray bottle and it will give back with beauty for years.

YOU WILL NEED

Clear glass container with an opening large enough to insert plants

Gloves

Clean ½- to ¾-inch pebbles

Bowl

Dried sphagnum moss

Dowel for tamping

Moistened potting soil

Wooden spoon

Terrarium plants such as ferns, mini philodendrons, and palm seedlings

Oversize tweezers

Lichen, stones, driftwood, twigs, shells, and/or other bits of nature

Figurines (let your fantasy flow!)

Turkey baster or small measuring cup with a spout

1. Insert a 1- to 2-inch layer (depending on the size of the glassware) of pebbles into the base of the container (A).

2. Fully moisten the sphagnum moss in a bowl, and wring out the excess water. It's important to introduce only a certain amount of moisture into the terrarium (B).

3. Insert a thin layer of sphagnum moss into the container and tamp it down with a dowel (C).

4. Spoon 1 inch of moistened soil into the container, tamping it down.

5. Unpot one mini plant (D) and massage the roots to loosen them before inserting the plant into the container with a pair of tweezers (E). Carefully place it firmly into the soil; repeat with additional plants. Be sure to leave some growing room between the plants.

6. Add soil to fill in gaps, and tamp it to keep the plants firmly in place (F).

7. With tweezers, insert lichen, stones, twigs, and natural objects. Add figurines to create a scene (G).

8. Add 1 to 2 tablespoons of water with the turkey baster or cup, and seal it with the stopper (H).

know your miniature plants

When making terrariums, the plants you choose can make all of the difference to your final gift, both in appearance and ability to thrive. Here are some of the best small greenery to reach for in these projects.

Spikemoss: (*Selaginella kraussiana* 'Brownii') Sometimes called clubmoss, this plant does best in terrariums or humid Wardian cases. It grows very slowly, so do not expect it to become a groundcover.

Silver sprinkles plant: (*Pilea glaucophylla*) Allow the top inch of soil to dry before watering, and protect it from hot afternoon sun. It forms a low tangled groundcover, setting down roots along the stems.

Polka-dot plant: (*Hypoestes phyllostachya*) Available in pink, red, or white, this is a favorite of fairy gardeners. Pinch the tips to keep it down to size.

Gray lavender cotton: (*Santolina chamaecyparissus* 'Pretty Polly') Aromatic gray or green foliage can be trimmed and shaped for small gardens. Very drought-tolerant when established, with bright-yellow blooms in summer.

Golden Japanese stonecrop: (*Sedum makinoi* 'Ogon') This bright-golden sedum enjoys gentle morning or evening sun. Hot midday sun will beat it down, though it tolerates hot weather. Drought-tolerant.

Wood sorrel: (*Oxalis vulcanicola* 'Plum Crazy') This non-invasive relative of wood sorrel shows off pink and purple leaves all the time, and it also sports bright-yellow flowers when in bloom.

Ripple peperomia: (*Peperomia caperata* 'Red Ripple') Available in burgundy or green, this little plant is a nice addition to a terrarium, growing to only about 6 inches tall. Soil should be moist but well-draining.

Dwarf ixora: (*Ixora taiwanensis*) This dwarf slow-growing shrub has a naturally rounded shape. It blooms repeatedly in full sun, but make sure it gets regular water.

Curtain fig: (*Ficus microcarpa* 'Tiny Limey') Leaves of 'Tiny Limey' are smaller than other F. microcarpa, and both work equally well for bonsai and miniature gardens. Prefers well-drained but moist soil.

Dwarf umbrella plant: (*Schefflera arboricola* 'Gold Capella') Schefflera make a nice choice for those new to bonsai. Water thoroughly after soil becomes very dry. Pinch tips to shape.

Asparagus fern: (*Asparagus densiflorus*) Not a true fern, this plant is more tolerant of dry indoor air than real ferns. Prefers bright, indirect light over full shade. Soil should be well-drained.

Coleus: (*Coleus* 'Tiny Red Toes') Upright coleus with small leaves make a bright focal point in miniature gardens. Some can be trained to a single stem by removing side foliage.

Mexican heather: (*Cuphea hyssopifolia*) This pretty shrub can be kept small with pruning, and it may be shaped into a topiary as well. Heat-tolerant. Regular water and full sun will keep it blooming.

Golden Monterey cypress: (*Cupressus macrocarpa* 'Goldcrest') Soft to the touch, this dwarf cypress needs full sun for bright gold color. Prefers temperatures 55° to 65°F. Allow soil to dry slightly before watering.

Variegated artillery plant: (*Pilea microphylla* 'Confetti') Perfect for humid terrariums or fairy gardens, this Pilea needs occasional pinching at the tips to keep the plant small. Look for the plain green-leafed version too.

Food Gifts

Few things are as satisfying to gift as delicious edible treats. So whether those on your list prefer sweet or savory, these kitchen creations have cravings covered.

149

serve up a soup kit

Transform a simple container into a gift with hand-drawn artwork.

YOU WILL NEED
Ceramic bowl
Permanent paint pen
Soup mix
Decorative trims
Cardstock

Draw freehand arrows around the perimeter of the bowl. Let dry according to package directions. Fill with soup mixes and add decorative trimmings as desired. Scan an print tag on Pattern Page I onto cardstock or thicker quality paper.

- TO A -
SOUPER
CO-WORKER

150
turn lemons into limoncello

Convert a few simple ingredients into an elegant Italian liqueur.

YOU WILL NEED

10 **large lemons**

1 **750-milliliter bottle vodka**

3 **cups sugar**

2½ **cups water**

1. Scrub lemons with a vegetable brush. Using a vegetable peeler, remove the yellow portion of the peel in narrow strips; measure 2 cups lemon peel. (If desired, juice lemons and reserve juice for another use.)

2. In a sterilized 2-quart canning jar combine the 2 cups lemon peel and vodka. Cover tightly and let stand in a cool, dry place for 10 days, gently swirling mixture in jar once a day.

3. Strain mixture through a fine-mesh sieve set over a large bowl; discard lemon peel. Return the lemon-infused vodka to jar.

4. In a medium saucepan combine sugar and the water. Bring to boiling, stirring until sugar is dissolved. Remove from heat; cool 30 minutes.

5. Pour cooled syrup into the lemon-infused vodka; stir to combine. Cover and chill overnight. Transfer Limoncello to sterilized half-pint canning jars or glass bottles. Seal and label. Makes about 7 half-pints. Store in refrigerator up to 1 month.

CRAFT IT

To gift, pour some of the liqueur into a screw-top jar, and tie a strip of corduroy fabric around the jar neck. Hang a manila tag adorned with an old-school label around the neck of the jar.

151

cheer up with cheesecake

This recipe makes 12 individual Brownie Cheesecakes that look like six cheerful snowmen when wrapped and presented.

YOU WILL NEED

- 1 28-ounce package cream cheese
- 2 eggs
  Nonstick cooking spray
- 12 vanilla wafers or chocolate sandwich cookies with white filling
- 2 ounces semisweet chocolate, chopped
- ¾ cup sugar
- 2 tablespoons all-purpose flour
- 1 tablespoon coffee liqueur or 1 teaspoon vanilla
- ¼ cup milk
  Caramel-flavor ice cream topping
  Honey-roasted peanuts and/or caramel corn

1. Allow cream cheese and eggs to stand at room temperature for 30 minutes. Meanwhile, coat twelve 4-ounce canning jars with cooking spray. Place a vanilla wafer in the bottom of each jar.

2. Preheat oven to 350°F. In a small saucepan cook and stir chocolate over low heat until melted; cool slightly. In a small bowl lightly beat eggs with a fork; set aside.

3. In a large mixing bowl beat cream cheese with an electric mixer on medium to high speed for 30 seconds. Add sugar, flour, and liqueur. Beat until combined, scraping sides of bowl occasionally. Stir in eggs and milk until combined. Transfer 1½ cups of the batter to a medium bowl; stir in melted chocolate.

4. Divide plain batter among the prepared jars, filling each about half full. Spoon chocolate batter on top of plain batter, filling each jar nearly full. Place jars in a 13×9×2-inch baking pan or 3-quart rectangular baking dish. Place baking pan on oven rack. Pour enough hot water into the baking pan to reach halfway up sides of jars.

5. Bake for 15 to 20 minutes or until puffed and set when gently shaken (cheesecakes will fall slightly as they cool). Remove jars from water; cool on a wire rack. Cover and chill for at least 4 hours before serving.

6. To serve, top cheesecakes with caramel topping and sprinkle on peanuts and/or caramel corn.

Makes 12 cheesecakes. Store, tightly covered, in the refrigerator for up to 1 week or freeze for up to 1 month. To serve, thaw in the refrigerator overnight if frozen.

CRAFT IT

Screw lids onto baked and cooled cheesecake jars. For a 2-jar snowman, cut off the toe from one baby sock and wrap the cut end with a length of twine. Glue tiny pom-poms to the ends. Slide sock hat over top jar. Make a small cone-shape nose using a scrap of construction paper; glue to the top jar. Stack to form a snowman. Adorn bottom jar with ribbon and pom-poms.

152

spice things up

This Spicy Southwest Rub is best on beef or pork.

YOU WILL NEED

- 1 tablespoon ground pasilla chile or ancho pepper
- 1 tablespoon paprika
- 1½ teaspoons packed brown sugar
- 1½ teaspoons ground cumin
- 1 teaspoon garlic powder
- 1 teaspoon ground black pepper
- 1 teaspoon dried thyme, crushed
- ½ teaspoon salt
- ¼ teaspoon cayenne pepper

In a bowl stir together all ingredients. Pour mixture into a glass spice jar; fasten lid. Attach directions for using rub to jar. Makes about ¼ cup.

To Use: Sprinkle about 1 tablespoon on 1 pound of meat, poultry, or fish.

153

go garlic-herb

This Garlic-Herb rub is best on lamb, poultry, and fish.

YOU WILL NEED

- 1 tablespoon dried basil, crushed
- 1 tablespoon dried thyme, crushed
- 1 tablespoon dried marjoram, crushed
- 1 tablespoon finely shredded lemon peel or dried lemon peel
- 1 tablespoon garlic powder
- 2 teaspoons dried sage, crushed
- 2 teaspoons fennel seeds, crushed
- 1 teaspoon onion powder
- 1 teaspoon salt
- 1 teaspoon ground black pepper

In a bowl stir together all ingredients. Pour mixture into a glass spice jar; fasten lid. Attach directions for using rub to jar. Makes about ½ cup (enough for 8 pounds of meat).

To Use: Sprinkle about 1 tablespoon on 1 pound of fish, chicken breast, lean pork, lean lamb, or lean beef; rub in with your fingers. Cook as desired.

To Store: If using fresh lemon peel, store rub in an airtight container in the refrigerator up to 1 week or freeze up to 1 month. If using dried lemon peel, store in an airtight container at room temperature up to 6 months.

CRAFT IT

Reuse a pasta box by carefully undoing all glued flaps until flat. Cut the box into three horizontal strips (top, middle, bottom). You'll need only the middle and bottom portions. Attach scrapbooking paper to box pieces using crafts glue. Refold the box with the printed side of the box on the inside and reglue the two separate pieces. The bottom will be boxlike and the middle will be a strip.

Reuse glass spice jars with lids by filling each with one of the spice rubs. Then attach labels for the rubs. Set the jars inside the box bottom and then slide the middle strip vertically onto the bottom of the box, creating a handle. Add a ribbon and a gift tag.

154
roast spicy almonds

Give a perfect snack to pair with bubbly or beer—a container of these Spicy Roast Almonds.

YOU WILL NEED

- 3 cups whole almonds
- 1 tablespoon butter
- 1 tablespoon olive oil
- 2 tablespoons Worcestershire sauce
- 1 teaspoon ground cumin
- 1 teaspoon garlic powder
- ½ teaspoon kosher salt
- ½ teaspoon cayenne pepper

1. Preheat oven to 350°F. Spread almonds in an even layer in a 15×10×1-inch baking pan. Bake about 10 minutes or until lightly toasted, stirring once.

2. Meanwhile, in a small saucepan heat butter and oil over medium-low heat. Stir in Worcestershire sauce, cumin, garlic powder, salt, and cayenne pepper. Drizzle over almonds; toss gently to coat. Bake for 7 minutes. Spread nuts on a large sheet of foil to cool.

3. Place cooled nuts into a plastic bag; seal bag. Place bag in a clean recycled peanut can. Makes 3 cups.

CRAFT IT

Reuse a tin nut can. Adhere a strip of scrapbooking paper to the side of the can using crafts glue. Glue a sticker tag to paper. Place a cellophane bag in the can and fill with the mix. Tie with a ribbon and add a tag.

155
bake fruited granola

A healthy way to start the day is always a welcome gift.

YOU WILL NEED

- ⅔ cup pure maple syrup
- ¼ cup olive oil
- 1 tablespoon vanilla
- 3½ cups regular rolled oats
- ½ cup toasted wheat germ
- ½ cup flaked coconut
- ½ cup pecans, almonds, and/or walnuts, chopped
- ⅓ cup flaxseed meal
- ¼ cup sesame seeds
- 1 cup snipped dried apricots or dried blueberries

1. Preheat oven to 225°F. In a small saucepan combine maple syrup and oil. Bring just to a simmer over high heat; remove from heat. Stir in vanilla.

2. In a large roasting pan stir together the oats, wheat germ, coconut, nuts, flaxseed meal, and sesame seeds. Drizzle syrup mixture over the oat mixture; stir to combine.

3. Bake for 1½ to 1¾ hours or until lightly toasted, stirring twice. Stir in dried fruit. Transfer mixture to a large sheet of foil; cool completely.

4. Place granola in a clean recycled plastic produce container. Makes about 8 cups.

CRAFT IT

Reuse a plastic produce container with a lid and a pasta box. Carefully undo all glued flaps on a pasta box until flat. Refold the box with the printed portion of the box on the inside. Using a crafts knife, cut a strip from the box. Wrap the strip around the container, then glue the strip together. Cut a strip of scrapbooking paper and glue around the center of the box strip. Wrap string around the center and attach a sticker tag.

get saucy

A slow simmer on the stove turns apples into homemade applesauce that can be enjoyed all year long.

YOU WILL NEED

- **8 pounds tart cooking apples (about 24 medium)**
- **2 cups water**
- **2 cinnamon sticks (optional)**
- **¾ to 1¼ cups pure maple syrup**

1. Core and quarter apples. In an 8- to 10-quart heavy pot combine apples, the water, and, it desired, cinnamon sticks. Bring to boiling; reduce heat. Cover and simmer for 25 to 35 minutes or until apples are very tender, stirring often.

2. Remove and discard cinnamon, if used. Press apples through a food mill or sieve. Return pulp to pot. Stir in enough of the maple syrup to sweeten as desired. If necessary, stir in an additional ½ to 1 cup water to make desired consistency. Bring to boiling, stirring constantly.

3. Ladle hot applesauce into hot, sterilized pint or quart canning jars, leaving a ½-inch headspace. Wipe the jar rims and fasten lids. Process filled jars in a boiling-water canner for 15 minutes for pints or 20 minutes for quarts (start timing when water returns to boil). Remove jars from canner; cool on wire racks. Makes 6 pint or 3 quart jars.

Browned Butter-Sage Applesauce: In a small saucepan heat 1 cup butter over low heat until melted. Continue heating until butter turns a light golden brown. Remove from heat. Prepare applesauce as directed, except do not add the cinnamon and stir the browned butter and

½ cup snipped fresh sage in with the maple syrup.

Freezer Directions: Prepare as directed through Step 2. Place pot of applesauce in a sink filled with ice water; stir mixture to cool. Ladle cooled applesauce into wide-mouth freezer containers, leaving a ½-inch headspace. Seal and label. Freeze for up to 8 months.

CRAFT IT

Fill jars with applesauce or granola. Cut the sleeve of an old sweater 2 inches longer than the height of the jar. Turn the sleeve inside out and stitch the cut end closed. Turn the sleeve right side out and slide it over the jar. Tape a gift tag to the jar so that the tag hangs out over the sweater.

157

deliver freshly baked muffins

Made moist with applesauce and shredded carrots, these Cornmeal Harvest Muffins provide a satisfying start to busy days during the bustling holiday season.

YOU WILL NEED

¾ cup all-purpose flour

¾ cup cornmeal

2 teaspoons ground cinnamon

1½ teaspoons baking powder

¾ teaspoon salt

¾ teaspoon ground ginger

½ teaspoon baking soda

½ teaspoon ground nutmeg

3 eggs, lightly beaten

1 cup packed light brown sugar

½ cup canola oil

¼ cup applesauce

1 teaspoon vanilla

2 cups shredded carrots (4 medium)

½ cup raisins

½ cup chopped walnuts

Chopped walnuts for topping

1. Preheat oven to 350°F. Line fifteen 2½-inch muffin cups with paper bake cups; set aside. In a medium bowl stir together flour, cornmeal, cinnamon, baking powder, salt, ginger, baking soda, and nutmeg; set aside.

2. In a large bowl combine eggs, brown sugar, oil, applesauce, and vanilla. Stir in flour mixture just until combined. Fold in carrots, raisins, and ½ cup walnuts.

3. Spoon batter into the prepared muffin cups, filling each about three-fourths full. Sprinkle with additional walnuts. Bake for 18 to 20 minutes or until tops spring back when lightly touched. Cool in muffin

cups on a wire rack for 5 minutes. Remove muffins from muffin cups. Cool completely on wire racks. Makes about 15 muffins.

Variations: To vary this recipe, use dried cranberries in place of the raisins, substitute slivered almonds or chopped pecans for the walnuts, and/or add 1 teaspoon finely shredded orange peel.

To Store: Store 3 days at room temperature in an airtight container or freeze for 1 month (thaw at room temperature).

CRAFT IT

Using a cardboard box bottom as a base, wrap a piece of corrugated cardboard around the base, leaving 1 inch of overlap. Hot-glue long ends together on back to create a slip-on sleeve. Place muffins in box, slide on sleeve, and wrap with ribbon. Add a tag and an evergreen clipping.

4 Ways to Embellish Food Gifts

158
tag a friend
Bend a sprig of rosemary into a circle and secure with a twist tie or fine wire. Glue a sage leaf or dried bay leaf to a gift tag; add a tiny gold star brad above the leaf to resemble a tree. Glue to thick paper adorned with ribbon

159
use your noodle
Brush bow-tie pasta with glue, cover with gold glitter, and shake off excess. Let dry. Tie pasta onto narrow ribbon to use as a package embellishment or garland.

160
stick to it

Using a small foam brush, paint ends of four cinnamon sticks with metallic crafts paint. Glue together in pairs. Glue a plain pair together. Glue the three pairs to form a triangle. Make a loop of silver cording to hang the ornament.

161
trim a tree

Stitch a triangle tree shape onto cardstock using green metallic embroidery floss. To finish, glue a star anise with a tiny gold bead glued in the center to top of tree.

162
mix up marshmallows

Fluffy and sweet, homemade marshmallows are a true treat.

YOU WILL NEED

> Nonstick cooking spray
2 envelopes unflavored gelatin (4¼ teaspoons)
¾ cup cold water
2 cups granulated sugar
⅔ cup light-color corn syrup
⅓ cup refrigerated egg white product or 2 pasteurized liquid egg whites*
1 tablespoon vanilla
¼ teaspoon salt
⅔ cup powdered sugar
3 tablespoons cornstarch

1. Line a 13×9×2-inch baking pan with plastic wrap or line bottom of pan with waxed paper or parchment paper. Coat plastic wrap or paper with cooking spray; set pan aside.

2. In a large metal or heatproof bowl sprinkle gelatin over ½ cup of the cold water; set aside.

3. In a 2-quart heavy saucepan combine the remaining ¼ cup cold water, 1¾ cups of the granulated sugar, and the corn syrup. Bring to boiling over medium-high heat. Clip a candy thermometer to side of saucepan. Cook, without stirring, over medium-high heat until thermometer registers 260°F, hard-ball stage (12 to 15 minutes total). Pour over gelatin mixture in bowl and stir well to combine (mixture will foam and bubble up in the bowl).

4. Meanwhile, in a large mixing bowl beat egg whites, vanilla, and salt with an electric mixer on high speed until foamy. Gradually add the remaining ¼ cup sugar, 1 tablespoon at a time, beating until stiff peaks form (tips stand straight). With the mixer running on high speed, gradually add gelatin mixture to egg white mixture, beating for 5 to 7 minutes or until thick (the consistency of thick, pourable cake batter). Quickly and gently spread marshmallow mixture into the prepared baking pan. Coat another piece of plastic wrap with cooking spray; place, coated side down, over mixture in pan. Chill at least 5 hours or until marshmallows are firm.

5. In a small bowl stir together powdered sugar and cornstarch; sprinkle about one-fourth of the mixture onto a large cutting board. Remove plastic wrap from top of marshmallows. Run a knife around edges of pan to loosen marshmallow mixture and carefully invert onto the cutting board. Remove plastic wrap or paper. Sprinkle top with some of the remaining powdered sugar mixture. Cut marshmallows into 1-inch squares. (If mixture sticks, coat knife with powdered sugar mixture.) Place squares, about one-third at a time, in a large resealable plastic bag. Add the remaining powdered sugar mixture; seal bag. Shake to coat marshmallows with powdered sugar mixture. Makes 80 marshmallows.

*Tip: If you can't find pasteurized egg whites, use regular eggs and pasteurize the whites: In a small saucepan stir together 2 egg whites, 2 tablespoons sugar, 1 teaspoon water, and ⅛ teaspoon cream of tartar just until combined but not foamy. Cook and stir over low heat until mixture registers 160°F on an instant-read thermometer. You may see a few pieces of cooked egg white in the mixture. Remove from heat and place saucepan in a large bowl half-filled with ice water. Stir for 2 minutes to cool mixture quickly. Place egg white mixture in the large mixing bowl. Continue as directed in Step 4.

To Store: Keep marshmallows between sheets of waxed paper or parchment paper in an airtight container in the refrigerator up to 1 week or freeze up to 1 month.

Cocoa Marshmallows: Prepare as directed, except sift ¼ cup unsweetened cocoa powder over the stiffly beaten egg whites in Step 4. Gently fold cocoa powder into the egg whites with a large spatula before adding the gelatin mixture. Continue as directed in Step 4, adding the gelatin mixture and chilling. Reduce powdered sugar to ½ cup and add ¼ cup unsweetened cocoa powder to the powdered sugar-cornstarch mixture. Continue as directed in Step 5 to cut and coat the marshmallows.

CRAFT IT

Measure a piece of felt and a piece of cotton to make a 4×4-incih square with a 2×4-inch flap on each side; cut out. Adhere together with double-sided fusible webbing according to package directions. Trim all sides using pinking shears. Fold up flaps to make a box and stitch together using embroidery floss; hide floss on inside of box. Fill a clear cellophane bag with marshmallows, tie the bag closed with ribbon or twine, and insert into the fabric box.

163
get sweet on rudolph

This Decadent Hot Cocoa is richer than the average stuff, thanks to the addition of chocolate chips and marshmallows. Layered in a jar decorated to look like Santa's favorite reindeer, it makes a perfect hostess gift.

YOU WILL NEED

- 1 cup sugar
- 1 cup unsweetened cocoa powder
- 2 cups nonfat dry milk powder
- 1½ cups semisweet chocolate chips
- 2 cups tiny marshmallows
- Wrapped peppermint candies

1. In a bowl stir together sugar, cocoa powder, and dry milk powder; set aside. In a 1½-quart canning jar, other glass jar, or plastic canister layer ingredients in the following order: cocoa powder mixture, chocolate chips, marshmallows, and peppermint candies.* Seal jar.

2. To make hot cocoa: Remove wrapped peppermint candies from jar. Stir together cocoa powder mixture, chocolate chips, and marshmallows. In a large saucepan combine 2 cups of the cocoa mixture and 1⅔ cups water. Cook and stir over medium heat until chocolate pieces are melted and mixture is heated through. If desired, drop a peppermint into each cup and top each serving with additional marshmallows. Makes 12 (6-ounce) servings.

*Tip: Use a funnel or a piece of waxed paper or parchment paper that has been rolled into a funnel when pouring ingredients into the jar or canister.

To Store: Keep in a cool, dry place for up to 1 month.

CRAFT IT

Layer ingredients in a glass jar, then cut four 3-inch pieces of brown chenille stem. Wrap ends around a longer piece and tie on additional 1½-inch pieces of chenille stem to form Y-shape antlers. Bend chenille stems to finish antlers and adhere to lid using hot glue. Cut out eyes from white and black construction paper. Glue eyes and red pom-pom onto front of jar. Add a tag with instructions for making hot chocolate.

164

pack a sugar cookie kit

Give the gift of an afternoon of cookie decorating (without baking!) with this kit that includes sugar cookie cutouts, frosting, sprinkles, sanding sugars, and small candies.

YOU WILL NEED

⅔ cup butter, softened
¾ cup sugar
1 teaspoon baking powder
¼ teaspoon salt
1 egg
1 tablespoon milk
1 teaspoon vanilla
2 cups all-purpose flour

1. In a large mixing bowl beat butter with an electric mixer on medium to high speed for 30 seconds. Add sugar, baking powder, and salt. Beat until combined, scraping sides of bowl occasionally. Beat in egg, milk, and vanilla until combined. Beat in as much of the flour as you can with the mixer. Using a wooden spoon, stir in any remaining flour. Divide the dough in half. Cover and chill about 30 minutes or until dough is easy to handle.

2. Preheat oven to 375°F. On a lightly floured surface, roll half the dough at a time to ⅛- to ¼-inch thickness. Using 2½-inch cookie cutters, cut dough into desired shapes. Place cutouts 1 inch apart on an ungreased cookie sheet.

3. Bake for 7 to 10 minutes or until edges are firm and bottoms are very light brown. Transfer to a wire rack; cool. Makes 36 cookies.

To Store: Layer unfrosted cookies between sheets of waxed paper in an airtight container; cover. Store at room temperature up to 3 days or freezer up to 3 months. Thaw, if frozen, and frost as desired.

CRAFT IT

Fill a box with cutout cookies, prepared frosting in a resealable plastic bag, and decorating sprinkles. Scan and print label on Pattern Page 1 onto cardstock or thick paper. Decorate label with glitter glue. Wrap box with ribbon and attach label.

165
prepare for s'mores

Homemade graham crackers make s'mores just that much better. Break your favorite chocolate bars to fit into the acrylic box, tuck in the crackers, and top with purchased marshmallows.

YOU WILL NEED

- 2 cups all-purpose flour
- 1 cup packed brown sugar
- ½ cup whole wheat flour
- 1 teaspoon baking soda
- ½ teaspoon salt
- ½ cup butter
- ½ cup milk
- ¼ cup honey
- 1 tablespoon vanilla

1. In a large bowl stir together all-purpose flour, brown sugar, whole wheat flour, baking soda, and salt. Using a pastry blender, cut in butter until mixture resembles coarse crumbs.

2. In a small bowl whisk together milk, honey, and vanilla. Add milk mixture to flour mixture; stir just until combined. If necessary, knead dough gently to form a ball. Divide dough into fourths. Cover and chill about 1 hour or until dough is easy to handle.

3. Preheat oven to 350°F. On a lightly floured surface, roll one portion of dough at a time into a 10-inch square. Using a fluted pastry wheel, cut each square into sixteen 2½-inch squares. Place on an ungreased cookie sheet.

Prick squares with a fork.

4. Bake for 6 to 8 minutes or until edges are firm. Transfer crackers to a wire rack; cool. Makes 32 crackers.

To Store: Keep between sheets of waxed paper in an airtight container at room temperature up to 3 days or freezer up to 3 months.

CRAFT IT

Stack these delicious crackers in a 4×4-inch clear box with chocolate and marshmallows. Include star-embellished roasting sticks. Tie up with baker's twine and a simple label.

166
don't be square

Fudgy brownies are so much more fun as cutouts than squares. Make a decorating kit for a chocolate-loving friend. Add a few festive cookie cutters, your favorite holiday sprinkles packaged in cellophane bags tied with baker's twine, and a container of Chocolate-Cream Cheese Frosting.

YOU WILL NEED

- ½ cup butter
- 3 ounces unsweetened chocolate, coarsely chopped
- 1 cup sugar
- 2 eggs
- 1 teaspoon vanilla
- ⅔ cup all-purpose flour
- ¼ teaspoon baking soda
- ½ cup chopped nuts (optional)
- 1 recipe Chocolate-Cream Cheese Frosting

1. In a medium saucepan cook and stir butter and unsweetened chocolate over low heat until melted and smooth; cool. Preheat oven to 350°F. Line an 8×8×2-inch baking pan with foil, extending the foil over edges of pan. Grease foil; set pan aside.

2. Stir sugar into the cooled chocolate mixture. Add eggs, one at a time, beating with a wooden spoon after each addition just until combined. Stir in vanilla. In a small bowl stir together flour and baking soda. Add flour mixture to chocolate mixture; stir just until combined. If desired, stir in nuts. Spread batter evenly in the prepared baking pan.

3. Bake for 30 minutes. Cool in pan on a wire rack. Using the edges of the foil, lift uncut brownies out of pan and place in gift tin.

Chocolate-Cream Cheese Frosting:
In a small saucepan cook and stir 1 cup semisweet chocolate pieces over low heat until melted and smooth; cool. In a medium bowl combine two 3-ounce packages of softened cream cheese and ½ cup powdered sugar. Stir in melted chocolate.

To Store: Keep in an airtight container in the refrigerator for up to 3 days or freeze for up to 3 months.

CRAFT IT

Paint the sides of a tin lid (shown here: XL Rectangular Tin with Window in Silver, containerstore. com) with white paint and sprinkle with clear glitter. Paint icicles on window and sprinkle with more glitter while wet. Shake off excess. Cut out snowflake shapes from folded paper. Adorn with snowflakes and pom-poms as desired.

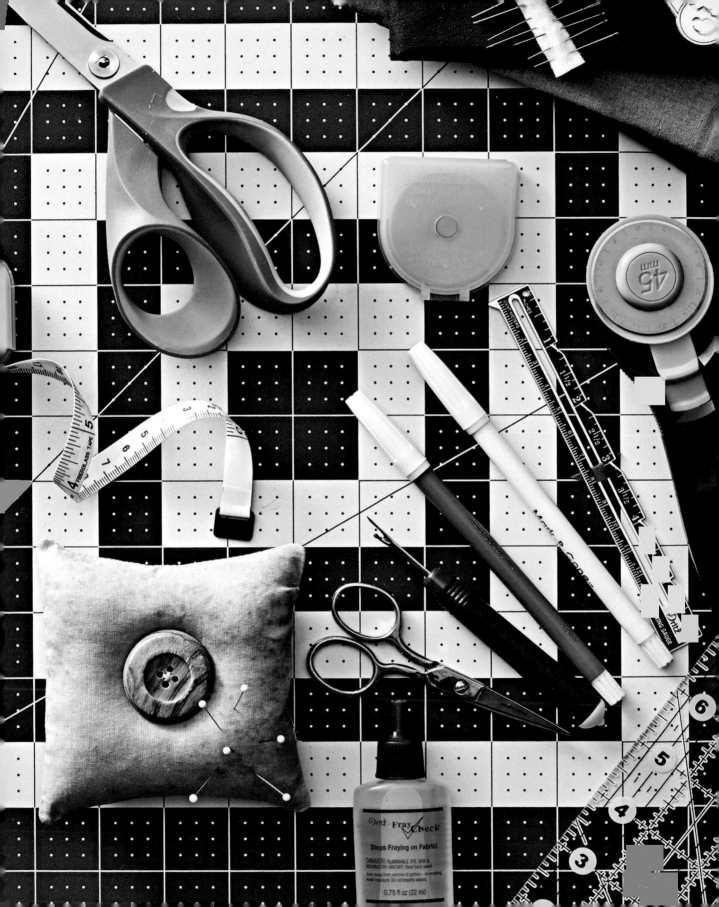

Crafting Basics & Patterns

Here are the background skills, techniques, and patterns you need
to make all of the projects in this book.

167
gather materials

Like any DIY project, sewing is easier when you have the right tools. Collect these items in a basic sewing kit.

Tape Measure: (A) Measure dimensional objects, such as pillows, with plastic or fabric tape.

Cutting Mat: (B) Use a self-healing mat to protect your work surface when using a rotary cutter.

Fabric Shears: (C) Reserve one pair of shears for fabric only—no paper cutting allowed.

Iron: (D) Keep an iron ready when sewing for crisp hems and seams.

Hand-sewing Needles: (E) Stock an assortment and replace when dull.

Needle Threader: (F) This handy little tool helps with the tricky task of guiding thread through the needle.

Rotary Cutter: (G) This pizza cutter look-alike cuts through fabric layers.

Sewing Gauge: (H) Use this metal ruler to double-check seam allowances when sewing or hem measurements when pressing.

Water-Soluble Markers: (I) Marks made with these are removed with water (don't iron over the marks— they may become permanent).

Seam Ripper: (J) Rip out seams and stitches when the need arises.

Embroidery Scissors: (K) Clip threads and seam allowances with these small sharp scissors.

Glass-head Pins: (L) Unlike plastic-head pins, these won't melt when touched by a hot iron.

Pin Cushion: (M) Keep one handy to keep your pins and needles tidy.

Magnetic pin cushions will help to find stray pins hiding on the on floors and carpets.

Seam Sealant: (N) Prevent raw edges or knots from fraying with this clear liquid.

Acrylic Ruler: (O) Roll a rotary cutter along a ruler to get straight edges and protect your fingers.

Note: After you've put together a basic sewing kit, you might consider creating a design wall or board. Having an area to lay out fabric choices or quilt block pieces can help you organize and visualize how they will look in your next project. For a more permanent design wall, cover a surface of foam-core board with a napped material, such as flannel or batting. Some sewers use the flannel back of oilcloth or a flannel-backed tablecloth for a design wall, rolling it up between projects.

168
know your embroidery stitches

Refer to these diagrams and instructions for the embroidery stitches used in the projects in this book.

CROSS-STITCH

Gaining popularity from charted designs stitched on the uniform squares of Aida cloth, cross-stitch works well for free-form embroidery on other fabrics as well. It's simply two straight stitches crossed at the centers.

To cross-stitch, pull the needle up at A. Insert it back into the fabric at B, bring it up at C, and push the needle down again at D.

CHAIN STITCH

Versatile as a decorative stitch, outline, or border, this clever stitch is simply a series of joined loops that resemble a chain.

To chain-stitch, pull the needle up at A, form a U shape with the floss, and hold the shape in place with your thumb. Push the needle back into the fabric at B, about ⅛ inch from A, and come up at C. Repeat for as many chain stitches as desired.

LAZY DAISY STITCH

One loop, similar to the chain stitch, is tacked down with a tiny straight stitch.

To make a lazy daisy stitch, pull the needle up at A and form a loop of floss on the surface. Holding loop in place, insert needle back into fabric at B, about ⅟₁₆ inch away from A. Bring needle tip out at C and cross it over the trailing floss, keeping the floss flat. Pull needle and trailing floss until loop lies flat against the fabric. Push the needle through to the back at D to secure the loop.

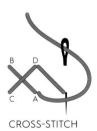

CROSS-STITCH

CHAIN STITCH

LAZY DAISY STITCH

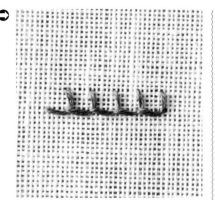

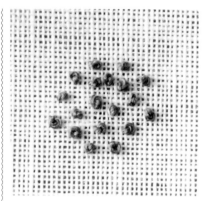

BLANKET STITCH

This decorative stitch can be a bit confusing at first, but with just a little practice, you'll pick up the overlapping pattern and stitch with ease.

To blanket-stitch, pull the needle up at A, form a reverse L shape with the floss, and hold the angle of the L shape in place with your thumb. Push the needle down into the fabric at B and come up at C to secure the stitch. Repeat for as many blanket stitches as desired.

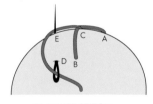

BLANKET STITCH

OFFSET BACKSTITCH

A variation of the traditional backstitch, this decorative stitch consists of backstitches that are slightly staggered.

To offset-backstitch, pull the needle up at A, insert it back into the fabric at B, and bring it up at C, slightly to the left or right of the first stitch. Push the needle back down into fabric at D in a straight line with C. Continue making stitches that alternate left and right.

OFFSET BACKSTITCH

FRENCH KNOT

This raised knot makes a nice dimensional accent when stitched alone, sprinkled throughout a design, or grouped to fill a space.

To make a French knot, bring the needle up at A. Wrap the floss around the needle two or three times without twisting it. Insert the needle back into the fabric at B, about 1/16 inch away from A. Gently push the wraps down the needle to meet the fabric, then pull the needle and floss through the fabric slowly and smoothly.

FRENCH KNOT

STEM STITCH

Just as its name implies, this stitch is often used for flower stems and outlines and works well for curved lines.

To stem-stitch, pull the needle up at A. Insert the needle back into the fabric at B, about 3/8 inch away from A. Then, holding the thread out of the way, bring the needle back up at C, half way between A and B, and pull the thread through so it lies flat against the fabric. Pull with equal tautness after each stitch.

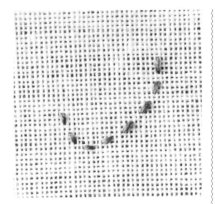

RUNNING STITCH

A simple stitch for borders and outlines, this stitch resembles a dashed line.

To make a running stitch, pull the needle up at A and insert it back into the fabric at B. Continue in the same manner, loading several stitches on the needle at a time. Leave about a stitch width between stitches.

RUNNING STITCH

BACKSTITCH

The ideal stitch for outlines, this simple stitch works best when a precise line is necessary.

To backstitch, pull the needle up at A, insert it back into the fabric at B, and bring it up at C. Continue in a straight line or to follow an outline.

BACKSTITCH

STRAIGHT STITCH

Sometimes all you need is a basic straight stitch, one stitch, stitched in any direction.

To straight-stitch, pull the needle up at A. Insert needle back into the fabric at B. Continue in the same manner.

STRAIGHT STITCH

SATIN STITCH

To fill an area with solid stitching, the satin stitch is the perfect choice and is recognized by its closely spaced straight stitches.

To satin-stitch, fill in the design area with straight stitches, stitching from edge to edge and placing the stitches side by side.

SATIN STITCH

FINISHING EMBROIDERY IN A HOOP

When all stitching is complete, turn the hoop over. Stitch a running stitch approximately 1½ inches outside the hoop in the fabric that extends past the hoop edges. Pull the thread to gather the fabric; knot the thread. Trim away the extra fabric approximately 1 inch outside the gathered line.

If desired, cut a felt circle that is slightly smaller than the back of the embroidery hoop. Stitch the felt circle to the gathered fabric on the back side of the hoop.

169
learn how to crochet

Here you'll find abbreviations, stitch details, and other helpful information to get you started crocheting.

slip knot

1. Make a loop, then hook another loop through it (A).

2. Tighten gently, and slide knot up to hook (B).

chain stitch (ch)

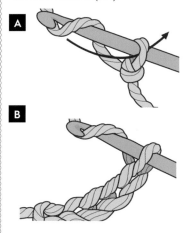

1. Yarn over (yo) the hook, and draw yarn through to form a new loop without tightening previous one (A).

2. Repeat to form as many chain stitches as required. Do not count slip knot as a chain stitch (B).

slip stitch (sl st)

This is the shortest crochet stitch and, unlike other stitches, is not used on its own to produce a fabric. It is used for joining, shaping, and—where necessary—carrying the yarn to another part of the fabric for the next stage.

1. Insert hook into work (second chain from hook on the starting chain), yarn over, and draw yarn through both work and loop on hook in one movement.

2. To join chains into ring with slip stitch, insert hook into first chain, yarn over, and draw through both work and yarn on hook in one movement.

single crochet (sc)

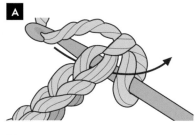

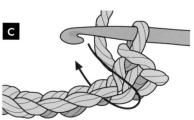

1. Insert the hook into the work (second chain from the hook on the starting chain) (A).

2. Yarn over the hook, and draw yarn through the work only—two loops are on the hook.

3. Yarn over the hook again, and draw yarn through both loops on the hook—one single crochet made (B).

4. Repeat from Step 1, working in the next stitch (C).

half double crochet (hdc)

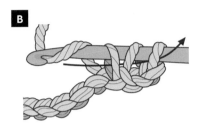

1. Yarn over the hook, and insert the hook into the work (third chain from the starting chain) (A).

2. Yarn over the hook, and draw it through the work only—three loops are on the hook.

3. Yarn over the hook again, and draw through all three loops on the hook (B)—one half double crochet made (C).

4. Repeat from Step 1, working in the next stitch.

double crochet (dc)

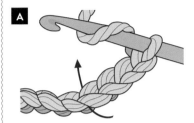

1. Yarn over the hook, and insert the hook into the work (fourth chain from hook on the starting chain) (A).

2. Yarn over the hook, and draw it through work only—three loops are on the hook.

3. Yarn over hook, and draw it through two loops only (B).

4. Yarn over hook, and draw it through the last two loops on the hook—one double crochet made (C).

5. Repeat from Step 1, working in the next stitch.

treble crochet (tr)

1. Yarn over the hook two times, and insert the hook into the work (fifth chain from the hook on the starting chain).

2. Yarn over the hook and draw it through the work only—four loops are on the hook.

3. Yarn over the hook, and draw it through the first two loops only—three loops are on the hook.

4. Yarn over the hook, and draw it through the next two loops—two loops are on the hook.

5. Yarn over the hook, and draw it through the last two loops on the hook—one treble crochet made.

6. Repeat from Step 1, working in the next stitch.

See next page for complete list of crochet abbreviations.

crochet abbreviations*

Abbrev.	Description
( )	work instructions within parentheses as many times as directed
*	repeat the instructions following the single asterisk as directed
alt	alternate
beg	begin/beginning
bet	between
bl	back loop(s)
bo	bobble
ch	chain stitch
ch-	refers to chain or space previously made: e.g., ch-1 space
ch-sp	chain space
cl	cluster
dc	double crochet
dc2tog	double crochet 2 stitches together
dec	decrease/decreases/decreasing
dtr	double treble
fl	front loop(s)
foll	follow/follows/following
hdc	half double crochet
inc	increase/increases/increasing
lp(s)	loops
p	picot
pat(s) or patt	pattern(s)
pm	place marker
rem	remain/remaining
rep	repeat(s)
rnd(s)	round(s)
sc	single crochet
sc2tog	single crochet 2 stitches together
sk	skip
sl st	slip stitch
sp(s)	space(s)
st(s)	stitch(es)
tch or t-ch	turning chain
tbl	through back loop
tog	together
tr	treble crochet
trtr	triple treble crochet
yo	yarn over
yoh	yarn over hook

*Adapted from craftyarncouncil.com

felt a sweater

Felting wool fabric brings the fibers in the wool closer together and gives it a more compact look and feel. The texture becomes more irregular and interesting. Always choose 100% wool fabric to felt. Sweaters that are nearly 100% wool will work, but the fibers will not be as tight. Sweaters that have less than 90% wool will not work well. Place the wool inside an old pillowcase to prevent any tiny fibers from washing out. Then wash the wool in a hot-water-wash, cool-rinse cycle with a little laundry detergent. Agitation of the wool loosens fibers and helps shrink the wool. Dry the wool in a hot dryer to shrink the maximum amount.

Press the wool with a press cloth if desired. Tightly felted wool does not ravel, and edges and seams can usually be left raw or unfinished, similar to purchased felt.

Patterns

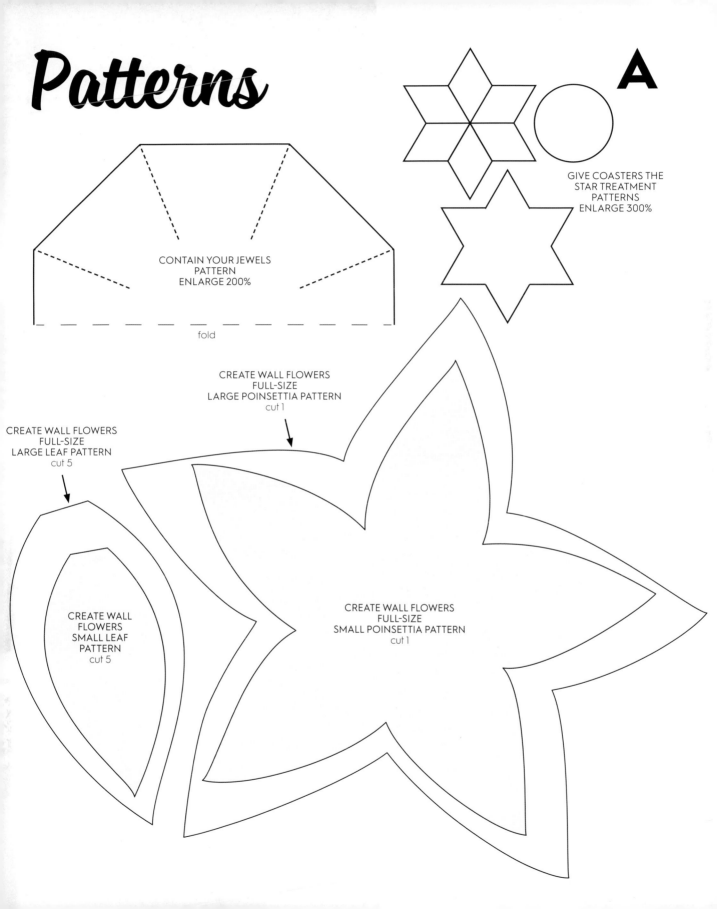

A

GIVE COASTERS THE
STAR TREATMENT
PATTERNS
ENLARGE 300%

CONTAIN YOUR JEWELS
PATTERN
ENLARGE 200%

fold

CREATE WALL FLOWERS
FULL-SIZE
LARGE POINSETTIA PATTERN
cut 1

CREATE WALL FLOWERS
FULL-SIZE
LARGE LEAF PATTERN
cut 5

CREATE WALL
FLOWERS
SMALL LEAF
PATTERN
cut 5

CREATE WALL FLOWERS
FULL-SIZE
SMALL POINSETTIA PATTERN
cut 1

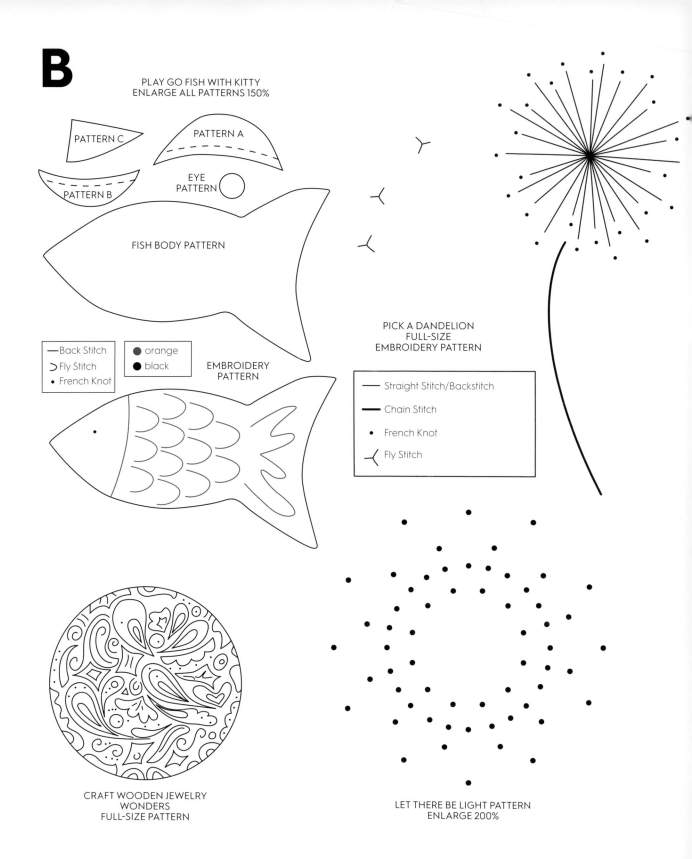

B

PLAY GO FISH WITH KITTY
ENLARGE ALL PATTERNS 150%

PATTERN C

PATTERN A

PATTERN B

EYE
PATTERN

FISH BODY PATTERN

— Back Stitch
⟩ Fly Stitch
• French Knot

● orange
● black

EMBROIDERY
PATTERN

PICK A DANDELION
FULL-SIZE
EMBROIDERY PATTERN

— Straight Stitch/Backstitch
— Chain Stitch
• French Knot
⟨ Fly Stitch

CRAFT WOODEN JEWELRY
WONDERS
FULL-SIZE PATTERN

LET THERE BE LIGHT PATTERN
ENLARGE 200%

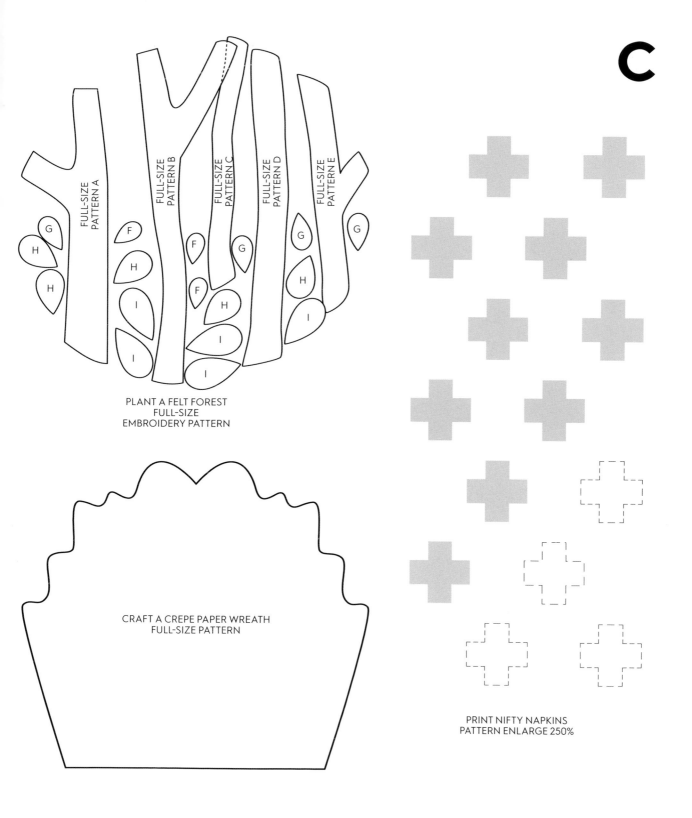

C

PLANT A FELT FOREST
FULL-SIZE
EMBROIDERY PATTERN

FULL-SIZE PATTERN A

FULL-SIZE PATTERN B

FULL-SIZE PATTERN C

FULL-SIZE PATTERN D

FULL-SIZE PATTERN E

CRAFT A CREPE PAPER WREATH
FULL-SIZE PATTERN

PRINT NIFTY NAPKINS
PATTERN ENLARGE 250%

D

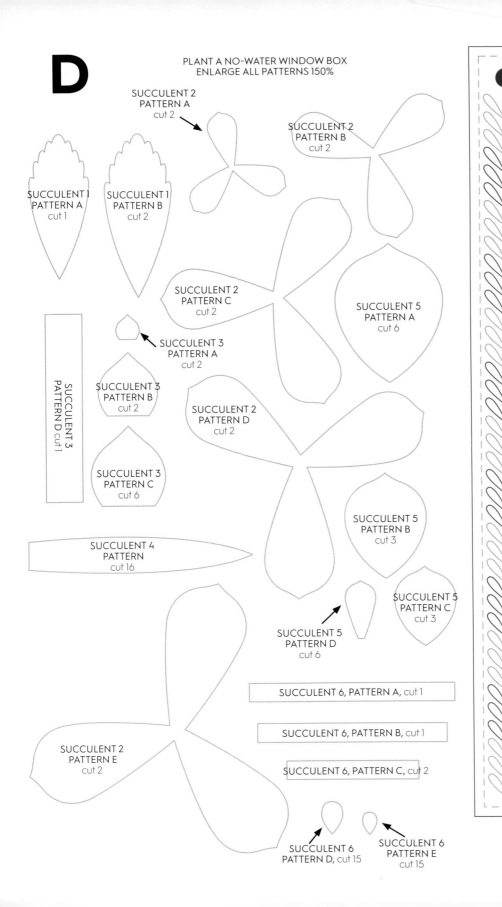

PLANT A NO-WATER WINDOW BOX
ENLARGE ALL PATTERNS 150%

SUCCULENT 2
PATTERN A
cut 2

SUCCULENT 2
PATTERN B
cut 2

SUCCULENT 1
PATTERN A
cut 1

SUCCULENT 1
PATTERN B
cut 2

SUCCULENT 2
PATTERN C
cut 2

SUCCULENT 5
PATTERN A
cut 6

SUCCULENT 3
PATTERN A
cut 2

SUCCULENT 3
PATTERN D cut 1

SUCCULENT 3
PATTERN B
cut 2

SUCCULENT 2
PATTERN D
cut 2

SUCCULENT 3
PATTERN C
cut 6

SUCCULENT 5
PATTERN B
cut 3

SUCCULENT 4
PATTERN
cut 16

SUCCULENT 5
PATTERN C
cut 3

SUCCULENT 5
PATTERN D
cut 6

SUCCULENT 6, PATTERN A, cut 1

SUCCULENT 6, PATTERN B, cut 1

SUCCULENT 6, PATTERN C, cut 2

SUCCULENT 2
PATTERN E
cut 2

SUCCULENT 6
PATTERN D, cut 15

SUCCULENT 6
PATTERN E
cut 15

CUFF YOURSELF WITH
CHEVRONS
FULL-SIZE
EMBROIDERY PATTERN

DMC COLORS:

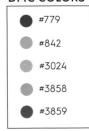

- #779
- #842
- #3024
- #3858
- #3859

- - - Running Stitch

⬭ Lazy Daisy Stitch

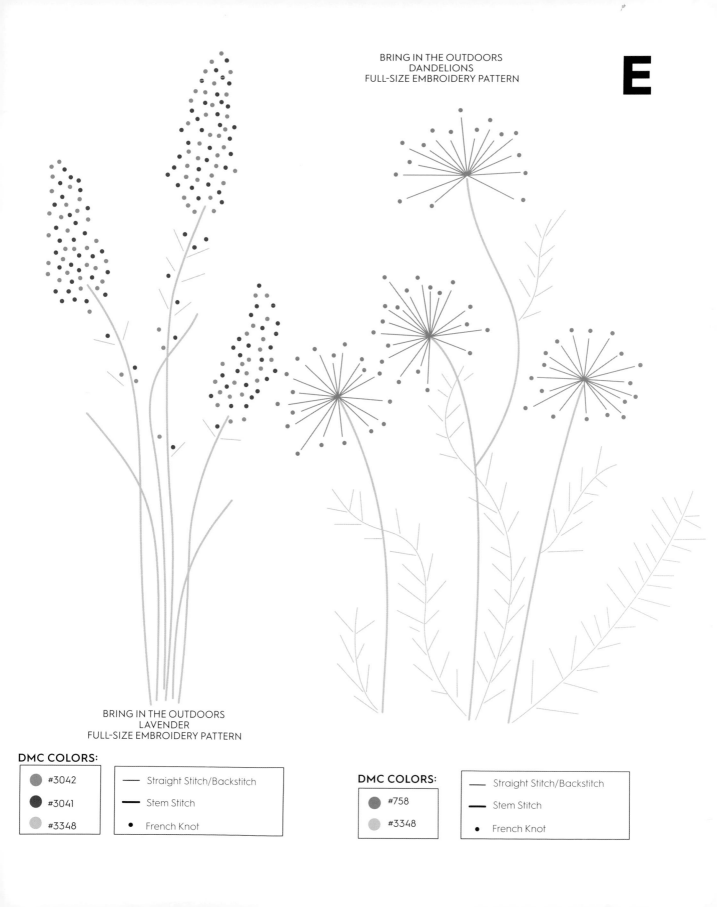

BRING IN THE OUTDOORS
DANDELIONS
FULL-SIZE EMBROIDERY PATTERN

E

BRING IN THE OUTDOORS
LAVENDER
FULL-SIZE EMBROIDERY PATTERN

DMC COLORS:

●	#3042	— Straight Stitch/Backstitch
●	#3041	— Stem Stitch
●	#3348	• French Knot

DMC COLORS:

●	#758	— Straight Stitch/Backstitch
●	#3348	— Stem Stitch
		• French Knot

F

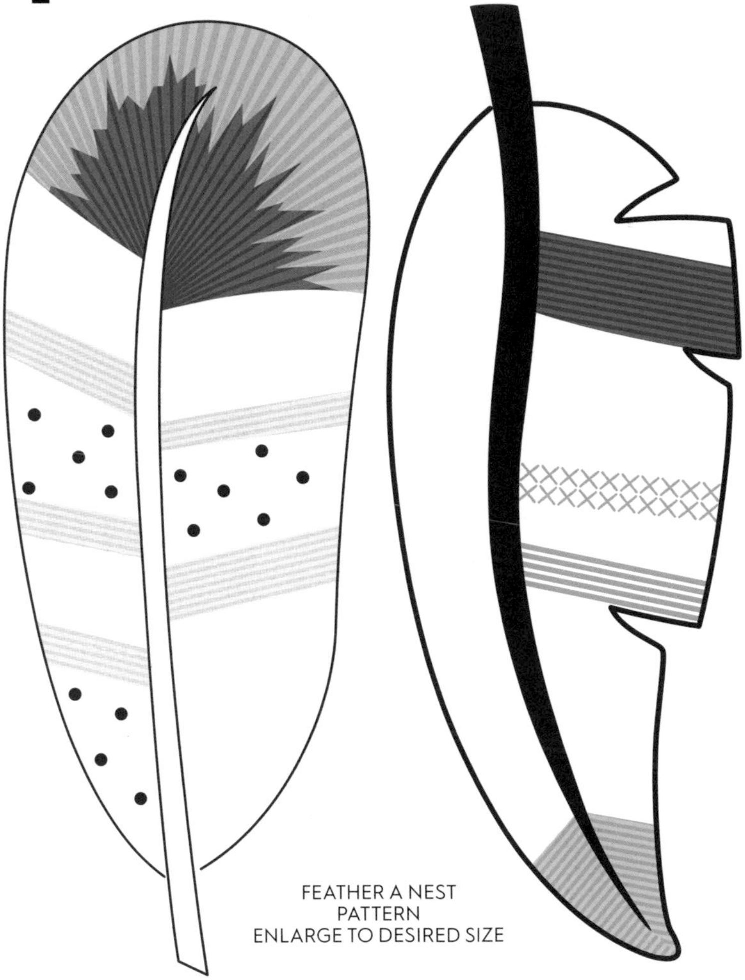

A · · · · · · · · · B

A · · · · · · · · · B

FEATHER A NEST
PATTERN
ENLARGE TO DESIRED SIZE

——	Backstitch
▬	Split Stitch
■	Fill with Split Stitch
▨	Fill with Satin Stitch
✕	Cross-Stitch
•	French Knot

○	White
●	Navy
●	Dark Coral
●	Light Coral
●	Yellow
●	Light Blue

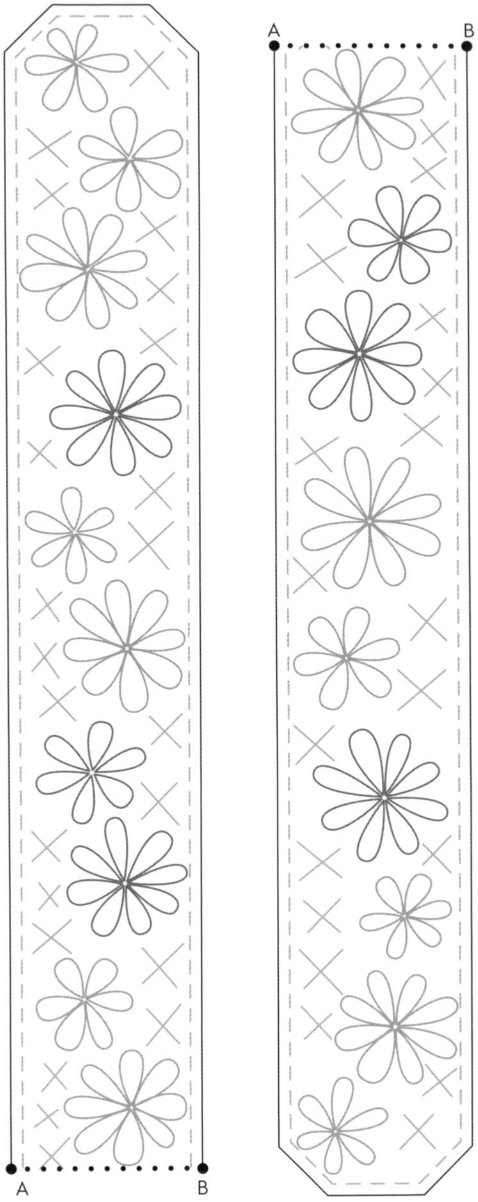

DMC COLORS:

●	#504
●	#842
●	#3024
●	#3778

---	Running Stitch
⬭	Lazy Daisy Stitch
✕	Cross-Stitch

57w×55h

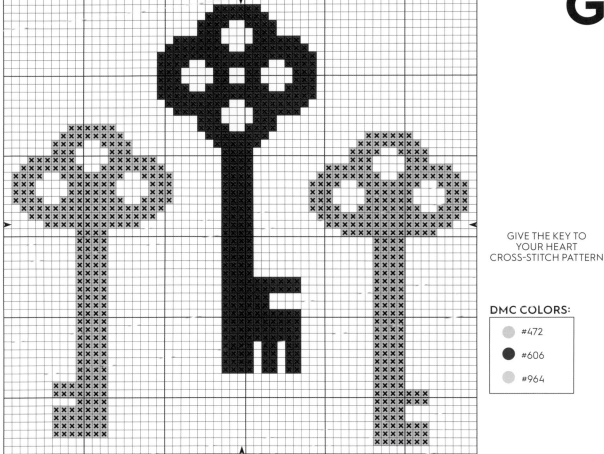

GIVE THE KEY TO
YOUR HEART
CROSS-STITCH PATTERN

DMC COLORS:

●	#472
●	#606
●	#964

H

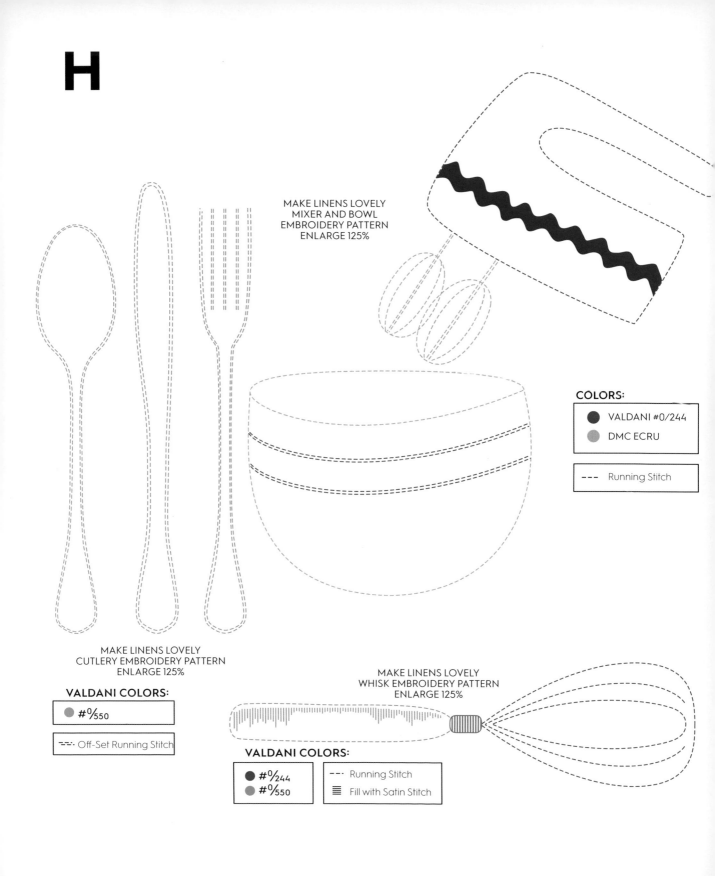

MAKE LINENS LOVELY
MIXER AND BOWL
EMBROIDERY PATTERN
ENLARGE 125%

COLORS:

● VALDANI #0/244
● DMC ECRU

--- Running Stitch

MAKE LINENS LOVELY
CUTLERY EMBROIDERY PATTERN
ENLARGE 125%

VALDANI COLORS:

● #0/550

--- Off-Set Running Stitch

MAKE LINENS LOVELY
WHISK EMBROIDERY PATTERN
ENLARGE 125%

VALDANI COLORS:

● #0/244
● #0/550

--- Running Stitch
≣ Fill with Satin Stitch

PACK A SUGAR COOKIE KIT
FULL-SIZE LABEL

- TO A -
SOUPER
CO-WORKER

- TO A -
SOUPER
CO-WORKER

- TO A -
SOUPER
CO-WORKER

J

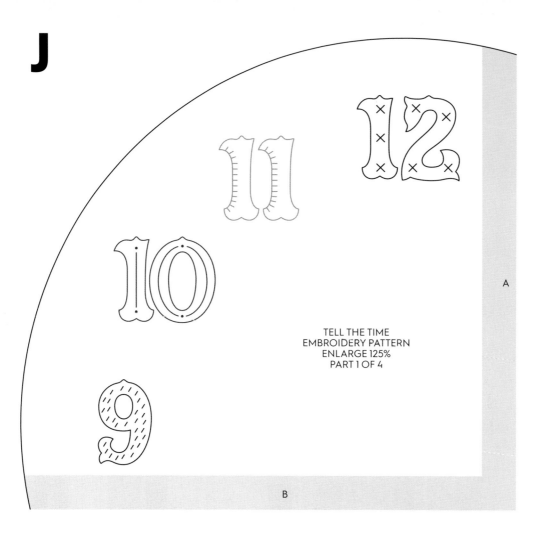

TELL THE TIME
EMBROIDERY PATTERN
ENLARGE 125%
PART 1 OF 4

A

B

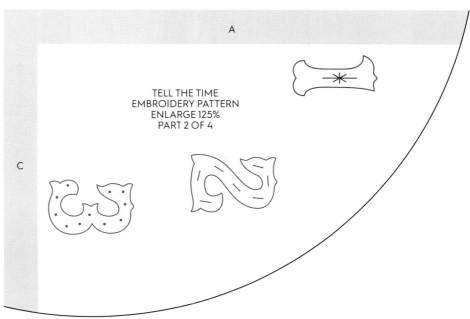

A

TELL THE TIME
EMBROIDERY PATTERN
ENLARGE 125%
PART 2 OF 4

C

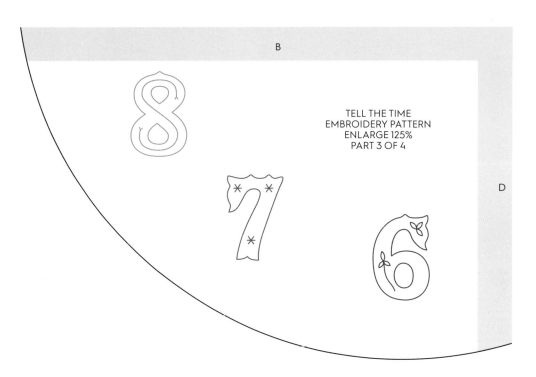

B

TELL THE TIME
EMBROIDERY PATTERN
ENLARGE 125%
PART 3 OF 4

D

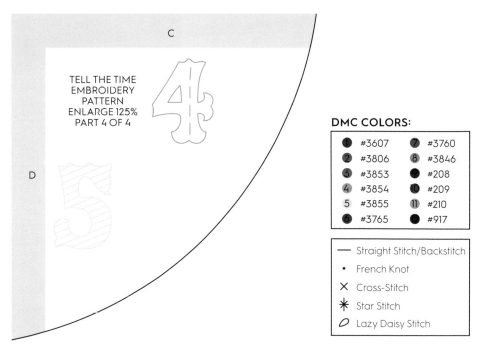

C

TELL THE TIME
EMBROIDERY
PATTERN
ENLARGE 125%
PART 4 OF 4

D

DMC COLORS:

❶ #3607	❼ #3760
❷ #3806	❽ #3846
❸ #3853	● #208
❹ #3854	❿ #209
5 #3855	⑪ #210
❻ #3765	● #917

—	Straight Stitch/Backstitch
•	French Knot
✕	Cross-Stitch
✳	Star Stitch
⟡	Lazy Daisy Stitch

Index

METRIC CONVERSION CHART

IMPERIAL	METRIC
⅛ inch	3 mm
¼ inch	6 mm
⅜ inch	9.5 mm
½ inch	13 mm
⅝ inch	16 mm
¾ inch	19 mm
1 inch	2.5 cm
1 foot	30.5 cm
1 yard	0.91 m
300°F	150°C
325°F	160°C
350°F	180°C
375°F	190°C
400°F	200°C
425°F	220°C
450°F	230°C
475°F	240°C
500°F	260°C

weldon**owen**

PRESIDENT & PUBLISHER Roger Shaw
SVP, SALES & MARKETING Amy Kaneko

SENIOR EDITOR Lucie Parker
EDITORIAL ASSISTANT Molly O'Neil Stewart

CREATIVE DIRECTOR Kelly Booth
ART DIRECTOR Lorraine Rath
SENIOR PRODUCTION DESIGNER Rachel Lopez Metzger

ASSOCIATE PRODUCTION DIRECTOR Michelle Duggan
IMAGING MANAGER Don Hill

Waterbury Publications, Inc., Des Moines, IA
CREATIVE DIRECTOR Ken Carlson
EDITORIAL DIRECTOR Lisa Kingsley
SENIOR EDITOR Tricia Bergman
ART DIRECTOR Doug Samuelson
PRODUCTION ASSISTANT Mindy Samuelson

Meredith Core Media
EDITORIAL CONTENT DIRECTOR Doug Kouma
BRAND LEADER Karman Hotchkiss
CREATIVE DIRECTOR Michelle Bilyeu
Business Administration
VICE PRESIDENT/GROUP PUBLISHER Scott Mortimer
EXECUTIVE ACCOUNT DIRECTOR Doug Stark

All content and images courtesy of the Meredith Corporation.

© 2017 Weldon Owen Inc.
1045 Sansome Street San Francisco, CA 94111
www.weldonowen.com

Weldon Owen is a division of Bonnier Publishing USA.

Library of Congress control number on file with the publisher.

ISBN 978-168188-293-2

10 9 8 7 6 5 4 3 2 1

2017 2018 2019 2020 2021

Printed in China.